THE MOST COMMON TAX MISTAKES MADE BY SMALL BUSINESSES

LILY TRAN

EA, CTC, NTPI FELLOW

Disclaimer:

The Most Common Tax Mistakes Made by Small Businesses does not provide binding tax, legal, or financial advice. The materials provided have been prepared for informational purposes only, and are not intended to provide tax, legal, or financial instructions as a substitute for a personal consultation. The material herein may not reflect the most current legislative or regulatory requirements, or the requirements of specific industries, or of specific states. These materials are not to be used for purposes of avoiding tax payments or tax penalties that may be imposed on a taxpayer. Readers should consult their own certified and professional tax, legal, and financial advisors before applying the laws or their interpretation of the laws to their specific situations.

DEDICATION

I dedicate this book to my son Amir, my inspiration!

TABLE OF CONTENTS

ACKNOWLEDGMENTS

Thank you to my son and source of inspiration, Amir. The day before my final exam to become an Enrolled Agent, he said to me, "When you keep doing your best, you will never fail." I passed all three exams in my first attempt, and in less than 5 months!

Thank you, Sam Mezistrano, CPA for believing in me and encouraging me to become an Enrolled Agent. Your mentorship and support has been life changing.

Thank you to all my teachers and colleagues for educating me about accounting and taxes. A special thank you to Dr. Anthony Newton for challenging me to become the best Enrolled Agent I can be.

My passion for my work stems from ongoing support and encouragement from my community of Enrolled Agents, some of whom are authors in this book. You inspire me do my best in work and life, thank you.

Thank you to my incredible authors and experts who joined me to share wisdom and guidance: Kevin, Jim, Amber, Shawn, Peggy, Lynn, Ellie, Jamie, and Harley.

Thank you, my amazing team, notably Leanne Kabat, my Editor-in-Chief, Josh Burns, manuscript master, and Nina Barnett for designing the amazing cover.

Lastly, with so much appreciation and gratitude, I thank my husband, my son Amir and daughter Lucy for their deep love and support. I have reached many incredible dreams because you helped lift me up and make it possible. And to my dad, who inspired me to build my business and keep his legacy of service alive.

Thank you to all.

INTRODUCTION

Entrepreneurship is a path that millions of people are choosing every year for their main income as they transition out of corporate work, complete their education, or have a shift in their personal life that conflicts with the rigid requirements of a traditional job. The top drivers for becoming an entrepreneur include being your own boss, having control over when and where you work, and having decision-making power in areas outside your job description, all of which are not typically available to those working for a corporation or organization.

Owning your own business can be rewarding, both professionally and financially. However, a business isn't guaranteed to be successful just because the entrepreneur has a driving passion to succeed. There needs to be a solid foundation under the passion, so the business can be built to last. Most entrepreneurs invest a considerable amount of time, money, energy, and mental focus to bring a product or service to market, while juggling sales, marketing, operations, customer service, and fulfillment systems. The benchmarks for success are often measured in revenue and profit, but in reality, there is another side to the financial coin which is overlooked and underdeveloped that must be considered at the same time: financial systems.

When we talk about financial systems, it includes licensing, insurance, and all areas of tax responsibility. When it comes to taxes in particular, many new businesses fail to plan ahead with a qualified tax professional and as a result, they either overpay and lose money, or underpay and find themselves out of compliance and on the radar of the Internal Revenue Service (IRS) which can lead to audits, fines, and penalties. Proper planning and financial system setup can make all the difference for how much money you pay and how much money you keep, while being in full compliance with the law.

As a small business owner, there are so many competing needs, and the more complicated ones tend to be pushed away for another day, like setting up good tax practices and habits. Every day, thousands of hard-working entrepreneurs make tax mistakes that cost them money, time, and peace of mind. We want to help you build the best foundation for your business so you can continue to do what you do best, while knowing you are following the laws, rules, and requirements for sustained growth and success.

In this book, we focus on providing vital guidance for small business owners in various financial, legal, and tax topics to help you understand them in an easy and helpful way and guide you to make the best decisions for your small business. Let's explore the most common tax mistakes that small businesses make, and how to avoid the financial and emotional pitfalls so you can run a healthy, strong, and viable business built on a solid financial foundation.

MISTAKE #1: FAILING TO SET UP BUSINESS PROPERLY

BY LILY TRAN, EA, CTC

When beginning a business, you must decide what form of business entity you want to establish for your venture. The entity you choose will determine which tax return forms and filings you have to complete. Choosing the incorrect entity structure due to a lack of understanding is very common. It is important to work with a qualified tax professional to choose the best entity structure for your business and to ensure the correct tax forms are completed and filed.

The various business structure types include:

- Sole Proprietorships
- Limited Liability Companies (LLC)
- S Corporations
- Partnerships
- Corporations (C)
- Non-profit

In this book, we focus on business owners in the first two entities because this is where most small business owners start their entrepreneurial journey. Often, they start their business without advisors and experts, so they are more at risk of making costly tax mistakes.

Every state has a government agency responsible for authorizing the formation and registration of business entities. These state agencies have different requirements, forms, and fees, so it is important to know what your business structure will be so you can set up your business correctly from the start. Generally, the filing document will require the name and address of the business, the name of the business owner, and other details depending on the business entity. The two most common entities will be explored more below.

Sole Proprietorship:

A sole proprietorship is a simple entity to form and is a good option for those who want to test their idea before forming a more formal business entity. With this structure, you have complete control of your business and have flexibility to test various options of your product or service, as long as you are doing it on your own without partners, team members, or employees. As a sole proprietor, you do not have a separate business entity from your personal entity, for tax purposes. This means your business assets and liabilities are not separate from your personal liabilities and assets in a legal sense. Keep in mind, you can be held personally liable for the debts of the business.

An LLC:

An LLC is a state-recognized entity that may allow you to operate your business as a sole proprietor, however, there are other entities that your business might be better suited for, so consulting a tax professional would help you make the right choice in your setup.

One of the benefits for having an LLC include personal protection. Personal protection is one of the main reasons small business owners opt for this business structure, as LLCs protect you from personal liability in most instances, and, unlike a sole proprietorship, your personal assets, like your house, car, and savings, won't be at risk if your LLC faces a lawsuit or bankruptcy.

However, entrepreneurs with an LLC taxed as a sole proprietorship are considered self-employed and are required to pay self-employment tax contributions towards Medicare and Social Security, and they can't go public with an initial public offering (IPO) to become a publicly traded entity on the stock market. To learn about business structure options, visit the IRS website at:

https://www.irs.gov/businesses/small-businesses-self-employed/business-structures

Not Securing Your Business License, EIN, and Other Codes

One commonly overlooked area of business setup is in licensing, partly because there are so many layers to it, depending on your business, your city, county, and state. In fact, there are more than 100,000 different jurisdictions across the country, and each has its own required licenses and permits. Every business, industry, state, and city has a different set of regulations in place. Even if you start searching online for what you need, you might find yourself confused or even missing out on key licenses that your business needs.

Business licenses are formal permits issued by a local government agency to authorize individuals or small business owners to conduct business within the government's geographic district. A single business in a single location might require multiple licenses issued by multiple government departments and agencies.

. . .

Here are the top ten most common licenses entrepreneurs maintain:

1. **Federal** – Most businesses won't need a federal license. However, if you are selling products or services regulated by the federal government, you may need a license from the appropriate federal agency before you start. Some examples of these businesses include those in industries like agriculture, alcohol or tobacco, aviation, fisheries, firearms and explosives, broadcasting, mining, transportation, and imports from foreign countries.
2. **State** – States regulate a broader range of commercial activities than the federal government, so most entrepreneurs will need to have a business license issued by their state to conduct business in the state. Some examples of industries requiring state licensing include retail, restaurants, trades like plumbing and construction, and businesses in the financial industry and beauty industry.
3. **County** – Some business owners will need to have a county business license, especially if they require a land use authorization for a specific location. Also, the county can issue special event licenses for fairs, carnivals, athletic events, or other large, public gatherings.
4. **City** – Almost every city requires a business to be licensed by the city annually if you have a business based in the city and/or are conducting business within city limits. Some neighboring cities require you to have an active business license if you visit occasionally and conduct business, in addition to the city where your business is based.

5. **Professional License** – There are some businesses that require the person conducting the service to be licensed in their profession. These occupational licenses may include realtors; pet caretakers; food service providers; personal care service providers like hairdressers, barbers, and estheticians; and daycare/childcare and education providers.

6. **Sales Tax License** – This license may also be called a sales tax permit in some states. It is an agreement with the state tax agency that the business owner will collect and remit sales tax on items sold by the business. With this license, the entrepreneur is required to collect local and state tax in the state that issues the license, and then remit the collected tax money to the proper tax authority. This affects in-person and online sales.

7. **Liquor License** – Whereas most other licenses require paperwork and payment, this license has restrictions and quotas. The state legislature determines the quotas, typically based on the population as measured by the U.S. Census Bureau. Unique to this license is the opportunity for residents of the geographic area to speak for or against the issuing of the license.

8. **Health Department License** – This license is designed to regulate health practitioners to preserve the health, safety, and general welfare of the public. Some examples of businesses requiring this license include physician-led ventures, nursing, athletic training and recreation facilities, tattoo and body piercing studios, food processors, therapists, pharmacists, veterinarians, and beauty treatment providers.

9. **Reseller's License** – This license allows entrepreneurs to not pay sales tax when buying

products on a wholesale basis for the purpose of reselling them to customers. These licenses may be valid from one to four years before renewal and can be used to purchase inventory or ingredients for making new products. This license can be revoked if the small business owner uses the permit to buy items for personal use or uses the permit to buy items they need to do their business, such as photocopy paper, tools, or equipment.

10. **Zoning and Land Use License** – Many homeowners don't like the idea of a constant caravan of customers coming to their home to buy a product or service, and zoning laws are therefore in place to maintain residential neighborhoods for residents, and commercial areas for commerce. Receiving a zoning license means you will adhere to very strict guidelines about: advertising and signage allowances, parking and vehicle traffic, the number of employees on-site, noise levels, smoke, odors, and the proper handling hazardous materials.

Once you know what your business will produce or sell, you must secure the proper licenses to conduct your business—or face fines, penalties, or even forced closure of your venture. You can work with your tax professional to identify all of the licenses you need to operate your business, on the city, county, state, and federal levels.

If you'd like to start the search on your own, you can look for your state's governing department, and inquire about your specific business.

EIN (Employer Identification Number)

After you receive your business licenses, you will need to apply for an Employer Identification Number (EIN) through the IRS website. There is no cost:

https://www.irs.gov/businesses/small-businesses-self-employed/apply-for-an-employer-identification-number-ein-online.

The EIN is a nine-digit number that identifies your business for tax purposes.

This EIN is used in place of your Social Security Number (SSN). You will receive a letter from the IRS containing your EIN. This number will stay with your business until you cancel your EIN number to close your business.

After you apply online or by mail, you will receive your EIN number. You will need to take your business licenses and EIN letter to the bank to open your business bank account. This is very important. Commingling personal and business funds is one of the fastest paths to audits, fines, and complications with the IRS, so our recommendation is to have separate bank accounts for both, with proper income and spending tracking for your business account. Depending on your bank, you might need to supply other documents so check with your local bank before your appointment.

Business Classification Code

If you have an LLC or are a sole proprietor, you must file a Schedule C with your federal income tax return. This Schedule C form is where you report your earnings, expenses, and other information about your business to the IRS. On Schedule C, you are required to classify your business by selecting the appropriate six digit business code from the list of business fields (the current index lists over 1500 codes). For example, the code for a daycare worker in a childcare facility is 624410, found under the category "Health Care and Social Assistance," under the subcategory "Social Assistance." It will take some time to search for the best classification, but it is important to be as accurate as possible.

Some online articles suggest you can list *999999 Nonclassifiable Establishment* as your business classification on your Schedule C form if you can't identify the correct code for your work. However, we have found that this increases your risk of an audit. You can use the North American Industry Classification System (NAICS) Code tool to help identify the best code for your business, which can be found here:

https://www.naics.com/search/

Tax Tip

- Secure all your business licenses
- Apply for your EIN from the IRS
- Take license and EIN to bank and set up a separate business account.
- Know your business classification code to represent your business accurately on your Schedule C tax form, reducing audit risk.

About the Author
Lily Tran, EA, CTC, NTPI Fellow

Lily is the Founder of TaxUSign® —providing virtual tax help for whatever life throws at you™. Lily is part of an elite group of tax professionals licensed by the IRS as an Enrolled Agent (EA), a federal program authorizing her to represent taxpayers before the IRS when it comes to audits, collections, and appeals. She's a Certified Tax Coach specializing in tax planning strategies, as well as an NTPI Fellow.

Lily is a graduate of the University of Washington, and has nearly two decades of experience in accounting, tax, consulting, and advisory services for small business owners and corporations. She is a member of the National Association of Enrolled Agents, past Director of Washington State of Enrolled Agents, and past Treasurer of Washington State Tax Consultants. She has been featured in Forbes, Bloomberg Tax and Accounting, SUCCESS Magazine, and the Journal of Accountancy. She is also a co-author on a children's story book called *Meet the Spunkiez Heroes*™, with her son, and enjoys living with her family the Pacific Northwest.

Company: TaxUSign

Website: https://www.taxusign.com

If you would like a consultation, please book a session on the TaxUSign website.

MISTAKE #2: INADEQUATE BUSINESS INSURANCE

BY KEVIN BARQUEST

Insurance is one of the most important aspects of owning a business, yet it is often one of the most underinvested areas for small business owners. When set up correctly, business insurance provides peace of mind that your company is covered for common issues that businesses run into while accepting some risk for the rare things that you do not choose to insure. And, just like having insurance in other parts of your life, determining the amount of your deductible also plays a part. When you decide what amount of your deductible will be, it determines if your insurance will cover your loss or if you will choose to settle a claim outside of insurance. The larger the deductible, the more risk, but the lesser the cost.

When starting, it is understandable for a new business owner to be cautious with their spending in all areas of their business. While business owners invest in operations, staff, and locations to support their revenue goals, they often don't invest in adequate and appropriate business insurance, and that single decision poses a more significant risk to the business's viability if something happens. Please understand that the opposite occurs as well, where small business owners are fearful that they aren't covered for every little situation that may come up, which impacts their policies and payments.

Connecting with a knowledgeable business insurance advisor is essential. Still, it is vital to have a foundation for the various coverages and the minimum important points you need to know. First, we will discuss when to start looking for coverage and what is necessary for most businesses, essential coverage for specific industry categories, and optional coverage for consideration. Claims is another area that will be discussed, and we will learn about submitting a claim, or when it might be a better option to not file a claim. Lastly, we will explore different scenarios where people were left uncovered by skimping on insurance costs, and we will see how the right insurance coverage saved other businesses.

When to Start the Insurance Process

As an insurance broker, I meet new business owners as they are about to open their doors to the public, after they have already been in business for some time. These are not the times that you want to be looking for insurance. In each scenario, a business owner will rush, not ask questions, and not listen to the conversation carefully because they have so much on their mind. Do yourself and your business a favor and start the insurance process early on, well before opening doors. Benefits of beginning the insurance process early:

- Gives insurance the focus it needs to protect you and your business
- Your agent may connect you to other professionals
- Cost may lead to a reevaluation of product pricing
- Determine if your business is in a hard-to-place industry

The most important thing to understand when searching for business insurance is that there is no single solution for every business or business within the same industry. Many variables impact the appropriate coverages that a small to medium-size business needs, and over time the needs of small businesses sometimes change during the initial policy term.

Business Insurance Policy Types

When first exploring business insurance, you will probably come across a lot of terms that seem familiar but need clarification. First, when you get business insurance, you are buying one or more of the following:

General liability is coverage every business needs. This protects your business from bodily injury and property damage claims.

Commercial Auto covers all vehicles of a small business to include endorsements covering employees' cars while running errands for the company. Basic limits include liability, personal injury protection (PIP), uninsured motorist, towing, rental car, comprehensive, and collision.

Key Man Life Insurance is life insurance written on the owners or top executives with the company to help protect the company from their untimely death and the financial impact their passing may have. Another option for a newer small business would be to obtain a standard term life insurance policy with a beneficiary to whom you have given instructions in case of your passing to wrap up all of the business expenses.

Commercial Package Policy (CPP) is a package of two or more coverages like general liability, equipment breakdown, inland marine, commercial auto liability, and commercial property. CPP is a good solution, particularly for small businesses just getting started that do not need the more robust coverage of a Business Owners Policy (BOP).

Business Owners Policy (BOP) is business property combined with business liability with additional endorsements pertinent to your business need. Business Owner Policies help protect businesses with a physical location against liability claims, fire, theft, property damage, and even advertising injury. The other benefit of having a BOP is that they are very customizable depending on your industry and business needs.

Specific endorsements that can be added include data breach, cyber-liability, business income, and more.

Professional Liability, also known as errors and omissions or E&O, covers negligence, misrepresentation, and inaccurate advice when conducting business. Many types of companies need this coverage; a few include insurance brokers, real estate agents, accountants, and many more. If your small business does any of the following, you need this coverage: provide advice to clients, offer professional services to customers, or a contract requiring this of your business.

Cyber-Liability can be purchased as a standalone policy or an endorsement on a policy with some carriers. It is important to note that no matter how large or small a business is, every business with the technology of any kind is at risk of a security breach. There are a lot of costs that come with a cyber-attack or data breach on your business, including lost business income, costs to notify customers of the breach, costs for recovering data, costs for repairing computer systems, and more. Cyber-liability has numerous options to address specific needs of a business which include forensic investigation, litigation expenses, regulatory defense expenses or fines, crisis management, business interruption, cyber extortion, and more. As you can see, this little policy or endorsement is crucial coverage your business needs at the levels of coverage that best suit your business and financial needs.

Inland Marine helps cover products, materials, and equipment while it is transported to and from a job site or related to a business event. The vital thing to know about this coverage is that you have to make sure that you have enough coverage so that if there is a loss, the equipment or product is covered at value. Companies make a mistake here because they provide a low number to keep the cost of insurance down or do not complete an actual assessment of what dollar amount is consistently being transported back and forth.

Workers Compensation, also known as workers' comp or workman's comp, benefits your employees if they get injured or become ill due to working on the job. The benefits that your employees would receive include medical care, lost wages during recovery, disability benefits, and even death benefits in case of death on the job. Most states have their own guidelines for workers' comp but four are monopolistic, which means the state runs the workers' compensation programs and it is not a separate insurance that companies need to purchase. The four monopolistic states are North Dakota, Ohio, Washington, and Wyoming.

Top Optional Endorsements

Additional Insured extends general liability to a third party and protects them against lawsuits or damage to property.
Business Interruption is available as an endorsement to cover your loss of income due to a covered loss. Specifically, this may help pay for payroll, taxes, loan payments, and even a temporary location if yours is unusable.
Directors and Officers Liability or D&O is very similar to professional liability, however, specific to the directors and officers within the company. This covers their liability and protects them individually from losses and legal fees if they are sued due to their relationship with the company.
Equipment Breakdown does what it sounds like it would do;

cover losses related to broken down equipment used in the course of business.

Although there are a lot of endorsements available, these are just a few of the most commonly used to get you started. As I have previously stated, it is imperative to find a highly recommended commercial insurance advisor to help you understand what you are and are not covered for to ensure you do not have any surprise uncovered losses. Like with anything, there is a balance between risks and rewards; business insurance is no different.

Optional Commercial Auto Endorsements

Employees as insured cover your employees while they are using their own vehicle and driving a company vehicle during the business day.

Auto Loan and Lease Gap works just like it would for your personal auto insurance. This endorsement would be added to the policy, and if the vehicle should be totaled and you owe more on the car than it is worth, this coverage will make you whole again.

Rental Reimbursement again works as it does for personal insurance. In the event of a covered loss, funds would be provided by your insurer to get you a temporary vehicle while the claim resolves.

Commercial auto insurance policies have a variety of endorsements available and depending on how your company uses commercial policies, the above are common endorsements used by small businesses. You will want to connect to a trusted commercial insurance advisor as you add additional vehicles or drivers. Commercial auto insurance is not the same as personal auto insurance. What you think you might be doing well to set up your policy may not fully protect you in case of collision, theft, or damage.

Business Specific Insurance

Restaurants

Restaurants have unique needs compared to most businesses; they have many perishable products on hand, may or may not serve alcohol, constantly have people coming in and out of their facility, and many more unique scenarios. Due to the particular needs of the restaurant industry, it is imperative to have the correct type of coverage based on your restaurant's needs because each will be different from the next.

Restaurants typically will start with a business owner's policy (BOP) as referenced previously, plus additional coverages, which will vary depending on the number of employees, whether the restaurant serves alcohol, if it's dine- in or take-out, if delivery is involved, and the annual revenue. One policy that restaurants need is workers' compensation insurance to protect employees from workplace injuries.

Endorsements to the BOP include:

- **Employment practices liability** – covers issues around hiring, employment, or firing.
- **Water contamination** – Covers anything that happens to the drinkable water and your business must shut down.
- **Liquor liability** – Protects your restaurant against damages from a drunk patron who causes damage or destruction after leaving.
- **Spoilage coverage** – Protects against losses resulting in food spoilage, such as if the fridge breaks or your facility loses power.

- **Commercial property** – Protects against loss to the kitchen, dining areas, and all equipment and furnishings at your location.

Professional Office

Professional office insurance is one of the easiest types of businesses to insure. Examples of professional offices include insurance agents, college planners, financial planners, counselors, and many more. Professional offices have a low risk for loss and typically do not require a significant number of endorsements or policy types to be covered adequately. In most cases, the professional office has a BOP to cover their building, contents, employment practices liability, and general liability. In addition, most of these professional offices add endorsements or policies for:

- Cyber-liability
- Workers Compensation
- Professional liability

Auto Repair and Service

The auto repair and service business types will include tire dealers, auto repair, mechanics, body repair and collision shops, garages, sound and communications installation, and oil changes. This is an extensive category, and it is one of the US's top types of small and medium-sized businesses today. The base policy here should be the BOP again because it provides the package of coverages, including building coverage, equipment coverage, general liability, employment practices liability (EPLI), and more. Additional endorsements often add:

- Cyber-liability
- Workers Compensation
- Business income continuation
- Faulty work coverage
- Lost customer belongings

Claims

Claims are a hot button area for all insurance, whether it be a personal insurance policy or a business insurance policy. Before submitting a claim, ask yourself the following questions:

- Is there an immediate danger of further loss?
- Is anyone hurt or could be hurt from this?
- What is the possible covered loss?
- How will this impact your business over the next day, week, month, and beyond?
- How much might this cost to resolve?
- What is my insurance deductible?

This is a very oversimplified way to view claims, but it can be this simple for a business owner to stop and make this quick assessment to determine the next steps. If it is not apparent what needs to be done, call your commercial insurance advisor or agent to discuss what is going on. Do not call the carrier first because the advice provided will come at the expense of a claim on your policy, even if you intend only to obtain feedback on what you should do. This is bad even if they do not pay out because this can impact your ability to maintain low rates or potentially switch insurance carriers. Typically, when you change insurance carriers, you will need to provide a five-year loss run, a report that would now show this claim with zero payouts just for calling to ask some questions.

. . .

Scenarios

Various insurance scenarios could be shared showing situations where small business owners are covered well and take a financial loss because they chose to underfund coverages to save money. Review the following and apply the scenario to the type of business you are opening up. Use these as additional topics to discuss with your trusted commercial insurance advisor. These are real-life scenarios with details modified to protect the identity of the clients.

Smoothie Shop – A business owner was notified by a neighboring tenant that water was leaking from the owner's smoothie shop, damaging some equipment in the neighboring business that needed to be replaced. The smoothie shop owner investigated the leak and found a piece of equipment was not placed back over the drain correctly after service. The smoothie shop owner assessed the damage's value while discussing the scenario with their commercial insurance advisor. The result was that there was coverage available; however, it made more financial sense for the smoothie shop owner to pay out of pocket for this claim instead of using their insurance. In this specific instance, property damage would have been the type of insurance that their insurance would have paid out if they put in the claim.

Real Estate Agent – A real estate agent had been working with a client to purchase a home. In a conversation with this potential client, the agent provided what was determined to be legal advice on a home and was incorrect, leaving the client with no recourse per the signed contract. The subject was related to the client's ability to add to a house when the HOA clearly stated additions like what the client wanted to do were not allowed. If this agent had recommended that the home purchaser review the HOA documents with legal counsel, the agent's errors and omissions would not have paid out $34,000 for the client's costs to sell the home and move into a home that met their needs.

Restaurant – A restaurant owner started a policy under the premise that they would not serve alcohol. Soon, another restaurateur shared financial data about his revenue from serving alcohol at his restaurant. Without telling his commercial insurance advisor, the restaurant owner started serving alcohol, and nearly fifty percent of his restaurant's receipts were from alcohol. Unfortunately, his staff over served a client who then drove home and got into a collision resulting in the other driver's death. This restaurant was held liable with no insurance coverage to help them out. The owner also operated under a DBA for a sole proprietorship leaving no legal protection for him and his business. The business is no longer in existence, and the owner will be paying back retributions from this loss for twenty years from the court settlement. If the restaurant owner had discussed introducing alcohol to his restaurant with his commercial insurance advisor, his advisor would have updated the policy option to include liquor liability to protect against this exact type of scenario without devastating his family's financial future.

Small business insurance is for you, the business owner, to protect yourself and your business from financial catastrophe in case of a covered loss. You heavily invested money, blood, sweat, and tears into your business—make sure it is taken care of, as it is the lifeblood of your family. Do not remove coverages to save a few dollars. It will cost you a lot more should you need it, and it is not there.

Tax Tip

Interview several commercial insurance advisors to find the one that fits best with you. Don't settle for the first one you meet as you will benefit more from having a strong relationship with them.

About the Author
Kevin Barquest

Honesty, integrity, inspired, leader, and success are the words best used to define Kevin Barquest. Kevin is the owner of two successful companies: Insurance Alliance, LLC, and Barquest Homes, Inc.

He strives for greatness while having fun in hopes of inspiring his two young daughters to someday work with him and possibly take over the businesses. In the meantime, he is serving his clients and building value in his companies while he deepens his expertise in marketing, an area he is very passionate about in his field. Kevin is also investing time to develop plans to acquire long and short-term rental properties.

Outside of work, Kevin can be found on the pitch playing soccer or watching his daughters play soccer. He enjoys traveling with his girls and having fun trying new things.

Kevin Barquest

Insurance Alliance LLC

https://theinsalliance.com

Barquest Homes Inc

www.barquesthomes.com

Email: kevin@theinsalliance.com

Phone: 253-355-3001

MISTAKE #3: NOT HAVING A STRONG BUSINESS TEAM

BY LILY TRAN, EA, CTC

In the beginning, most entrepreneurs run their entire operation on their own; they research their market and understand their client's needs, then they create the product or service and do all the marketing, sales, fulfillment, and administrative work behind the scenes. When their business starts making sales and earning revenue, it becomes time to hire people who can help.

Oftentimes, entrepreneurs first hire people for front-facing roles, like sales and marketing experts, including designers to create a brand identity, logo, and marketing materials. However, hiring or contracting with experts who can help you build and strengthen the parts of your business your clients never see may be a better investment in the long run.

Think about it this way. If you had ten new clients show up to buy your $10 product, you would have $100 in revenue, which is great! If you do this several more times, you will be earning thousands and feel excited with all this new cash in your pocket. But in fact, you don't own all that money, and this is a mistake many small business owners make which leaves them at risk for fines, penalties, and sleepless nights.

27

Most likely, your business requires you to register and pay municipal, state or provincial, and federal taxes on a regular basis, as well as pay the expenses for running your business, staying current on any professional licensing fees, having sound legal contracts or agreements for your work, and maintaining business insurance. Since all these things are in the background of our business, it's easy to push them off your to-do list because your client relations or product delivery takes precedence. However, the cost and stress of not being in compliance from a tax and financial perspective is massive, so you need to have the right people on our team to keep all parts of our business, front- facing and behind-the-scenes operations – working together for your overall success.

Successful entrepreneurs and small business owners hire financial experts early in their venture, not just to organize payments and income, or to complete tax returns, but to act as a tax planner. Tax planning allows the entrepreneur to avoid making tax mistakes, and to make business decisions that reduce taxes paid, as well as use all of the tax rules and regulations to their benefit.

Do you know how to ensure you aren't overpaying or underpaying on your taxes? What about making sure you are taking money out of your business responsibly? When do you need a tax attorney? There are many professionals able to support small business owners but sometimes we don't know who specializes in what part of the business operations. Let's take a look at some of the top experts in this area so you can identify the right people to bring into your business to maintain compliance and support your company's growth.

Bookkeeper

A bookkeeper is a great early hire for your business because this professional can help you create and maintain your financial records and create a system for your business to track all of the financial components. They help document transaction details, put together financial reports, and maintain accurate records around the sales, payments, purchases, and revenue in your business, and can submit your tax payments on time.

Accountant

An accountant is someone who can take the data that the bookkeeper tracked and recorded, and prepare a company's overall financial statements like balance sheets and profit and loss statements, examine and analyze the business accounts, and ensure the company is in compliance with financial reporting. Other responsibilities an accountant might have could include reconciling the bank statements and the book-keeping records to ensure accuracy and filing or remitting taxes on schedule. Accountants are often skilled at doing a deep and thorough analysis of a company's financial accounts and offering recommendations for upcoming financial actions.

Certified Public Accountant

A Certified Public Accountant, or CPA, is an accountant who has passed rigorous examinations to be licensed in their state. In order to stay current on their license, they must complete continuing education courses every year. A CPA can provide more comprehensive services than accountants because they have more training and expertise in areas of financial reporting, tax planning, and financial services. These professionals can handle tax returns of any complexity, and they are versed in the tax code to help their clients stay in compliance while reducing their tax payments.

Tax Professional

Unlike traditional accountants or general CPA's who oversee their clients' financial operations, tax professionals focus solely on a client's taxes. This specialty niche in the accounting field is highly regulated by the Internal Revenue Code, which outlines specific tax laws that both individuals and businesses are required to follow when filing their tax return documents. When a small business owner starts working with a tax professional and the tax professional understands the financials of the business, they can provide expert guidance for reducing taxes while staying in compliance.

Financial Advisor

People in this profession are typically the most knowledgeable about financial markets, financial trends, and investment performance data because most of their training is in the investment and markets. Financial advisors are required to have a university degree and a professional license, and although they might not know the tax law or the tax code as thoroughly as a tax professional or a tax lawyer, they do have extensive knowledge in financial areas with tax implications, like investments, retirement planning, and annuities. Working with a financial planner provides you with education and guidance on the various products and services available to you to reach your financial and monetary goals.

Enrolled Agent

An Enrolled Agent (EA) is a tax professional who often saves their clients from serious tax troubles because they hold a unique credential that allows them to represent clients facing disputes with the IRS. They are specially licensed professionals who act on behalf of clients who are facing audits, asset forfeiture, or those who want to appeal decisions of the IRS. One of the key benefits of these professionals, in addition to their depth and breadth of knowledge around the tax code, is their ability to handle tax returns of any complexity and identify areas of a company's returns which are not in compliance.

U.S. Tax Attorney

These professionals are the ultimate tax experts, and tax attorneys specialize in the most complicated intricacies of tax law. If a small business owner is audited, or is called to tax court, this is the right person for this critical task. Tax attorneys must be a practicing lawyer in good standing and can specialize in tax law after earning their law degree.

U.S. Tax Court Practitioner

U.S. Tax Court Practitioners (USTCP) are qualified tax professionals who are not attorneys yet are permitted to present in the U.S. Tax Court. The exam is quite extensive, and it covers topics such as federal taxation, federal rules of evidence, and tax court rules, and it ensures that only professionals who possess the requisite qualifications are allowed before the court.

About the Author
Lily Tran, EA, CTC, NTPI Fellow

Lily is the Founder and CEO of TaxUSign®— providing virtual tax help for whatever life throws at you™. Lily is part of an elite group of tax professionals licensed by the IRS as an Enrolled Agent (EA), a federal program authorizing her to represent taxpayers before the IRS when it comes to audits, collections, and appeals. She's a Certified Tax Coach specializing in tax planning strategies, as well as an NTPI Fellow.

Lily is a graduate of the University of Washington, and has nearly two decades of experience in accounting, tax, consulting, and advisory services for small business owners and corporations. She is a member of the National Association of Enrolled Agents, past Director of Washington State of Enrolled Agents, and past Treasurer of Washington State Tax Consultants. She has been featured in Forbes, Bloomberg Tax and Accounting, SUCCESS Magazine, and the Journal of Accountancy. She is also a co-author on a children's story book called *Meet the Spunkiez Heroes*™, with her son, and enjoys living with her family the Pacific Northwest.

Company: TaxUSign

Website: https://www.taxusign.com

If you would like a consultation, please book a session on the TaxUSign website.

MISTAKE #4: JUMPING INTO S CORP TOO FAST

BY JAMIE E. O'KANE, CPA, CTC

S Corporations – Look Before You Leap

If S Corporations were prescription drugs, I would assert that there is a crisis of overprescribing to the level of malpractice on the part of tax professionals (and laypersons). That seems dramatic, but it's true. Every day I get a message from a business owner who hasn't made a dime but is somehow the sole shareholder of a shiny new S Corporation. These business owners are then shocked at the compliance requirements needed to maintain their S Corporation as well as the costs to do so. They have started their business in the red and it usually doesn't bode well for their longevity or cash flow.

What is an S Corporation?

S Corporations are corporations that elect to pass corporate income, losses, deductions, and credits through to their shareholders for federal tax purposes. Shareholders of S Corporations report the flow-through of income and losses on their personal tax returns and are assessed tax at their individual income tax rates. This allows S Corporations to avoid double taxation on the corporate income.

Basically, S Corporations are sort of a hybrid entity of a C Corp and a partnership/sole proprietorship. The S Corp takes aspects of both of those entity types and makes some of the compliance simpler and some of it more difficult. Welcome to the US tax code.

Most people establish S Corps as a 'tax savings' move but don't understand the compliance requirements they are taking on so, before we talk potential tax savings, let's talk compliance. I will walk you through the biggest considerations to understand before you leap.

Paying Yourself Can Be Complicated

Let's get to the most pertinent subject first – paying yourself. You are in business to make money and you would like to use said money to fund your business and, most importantly, personal goals. If you are a shareholder in an S Corporation you can't just take any and all available cash at any given time. There are compliance issues and considerations when taking every dollar out of the S Corp. There are a few ways to get money out of an S Corporation. Here are the most common:

1. Reasonable Compensation
2. Dividend Distributions
3. Expense Reimbursements
4. Shareholder Loans

All of these have considerations to understand before implementing—let's get to it.

Reasonable Compensation

S Corporation shareholders who work for or provide services to the S Corp are required to be paid a reasonable W-2 wage. This salary needs to be a proper and defensible amount that considers the roles, tasks, and expertise that the shareholder provides as an employee of the corporation. There are many ways to determine what a proper salary would be for each shareholder. Some of the most common approaches are:

Many Hats Approach – this type of analysis takes the roles, tasks, or "hats" a shareholder wears in the business, allocates them over the hours the shareholder dedicates to the business and then assigns a market wage to come up with a composite salary. This approach is most commonly used for small businesses whose shareholders provide a myriad of services to the S Corp.

Market Approach – this type of analysis determines the salary required to hire a replacement for the shareholders role.

Which approach should a shareholder use? It depends, but the goal here is always to determine the minimum salary that is reasonable and defensible in the event of an audit. Let's illustrate the difference between each approach:

The sole shareholder is a veterinarian with 10+ years of experience whose S Corp provides in-home euthanasia and end of life services in the Denver Metro area. The shareholder is the only employee, and they work full-time. Each week the shareholder's roles include bookkeeping, payroll, purchasing of supplies, scheduling appointments, driving and veterinary services. Each approach produces the following yearly compensation:

Many Hats Approach - $80,000

Market Approach - $117,000

In this scenario the shareholder has many roles that are valued at a lower market wage than their main professional role. The many hats approach takes these roles into account while the market approach does not. In this scenario the shareholder would likely choose to document the lower salary as their minimum reasonable compensation. The shareholder can always take more salary in the event they want to maximize retirement contributions, and looking to show more W-2 income for investment purposes, etc.

Takeaway: What would reasonable compensation be for each shareholder who actively works in the business?

Dividend Distributions

Dividend distributions are payments of retained profits, cash, or property to the shareholders. The S Corporation must pay the distributions in proportion to each shareholder's stock ownership. Failure to do so invalidates the S Corp status and reverts the entity to a C Corp. Hooray! Double taxation.

Every S Corp shareholder I take on as a client gives me a funny look when I say "okay, let me show you how to know how much cash the S Corp can distribute without creating a taxable event."

Then they ask: "I can't just take whatever is in the bank account?"

Unfortunately, no. Anytime an S Corp distributes cash or property in excess of a shareholder's basis (we will get to basis in a bit) in the S Corp, the distributions are taxable.

How does an S Corp have available cash in excess of profits? Debt. Debt such as credit card liabilities, lines of credit, operating loans and even shareholder loans to the S Corp create cash in excess of profits.

Property distributions are distributions of capital assets, inventory, investments, etc. These types of distributions can be complicated so I will just say: don't distribute property out of an S Corp to shareholders without talking to your tax professional.

Takeaway: Be very cautious when distributing cash or property to shareholders.

Expense Reimbursements

Shareholders who provide services to their S Corps usually have out-of-pocket expenses or personal assets they use for the benefit of their business. The most common are home offices, vehicle use, licenses, travel, etc. Because S Corp shareholders are also employees, these expenses must be properly reimbursed to be deductible. Enter the accountable reimbursement plan.

An accountable reimbursement plan is a plan that qualifies under IRS regulations to not be included in the employee's taxable income. These plans require that all expenses be legitimate business expenses and they be documented (receipts, mileage logs, etc.). When qualifications are met, the reimbursement dollars are tax free.

Takeaway: Establish an accountable plan to be paid tax free dollars from your S Corp.

Shareholder Loans

Shareholders and their S Corps can loan each other money. These transactions have certain requirements to make sure they are legitimate loans instead of compensation to the shareholder, distributions, contributions, gifts, etc. These requirements include:

- a contract with a stated interest rate
- a specified length of time for repayment
- a consequence for failure to repay the loan

If a transaction is truly a loan, it should look and act like any other business loan.

Takeaway: Loan contracts are always a good idea.

Shareholder Basis & Why It's Required

Basis is the value of a shareholder's investment or stock at a given time. Basis is used for tax purposes to determine: if dividend distributions are taxable, if the shareholder can deduct losses, and to determine gain or loss on investments in a sale.

Up until recently, basis was required to be tracked by the shareholder in their record keeping and wasn't required to be included in their tax filings. This requirement is one of the most overlooked compliance pieces by shareholders and, unfortunately, their tax professionals.

As of 2018, the IRS now requires basis schedules to be included with the personal tax return any time a shareholder reports a loss, receives a distribution, disposes of stock, or receives a loan payment.

Takeaway: S Corp shareholders must track their basis and report it.

Bookkeeping, Payroll & Tax Filings

Bookkeeping

Bookkeeping is an essential part of running any business, but it is especially important when maintaining an S Corporation. S Corps are entities separate from their shareholders and therefore documenting each transaction properly for reporting and compliance purposes is of the utmost importance. Proper books and records inform tax filings, lending decisions, available capital and managerial decisions.

The elements of a proper bookkeeping system are bookkeeping software, frequent updating, record retention & periodic verification of balances.

Bookkeeping software – this is the cornerstone of any bookkeeping system. Software maintains double-entry accounting for each transaction which then enables solid financial reporting.

Frequent updating – bookkeeping should not be a once-a-year task; monthly updates and reconciliations help maintain balances, understand trends, and help make informed decisions.

Record Retention – all businesses should maintain receipts, invoices, purchase orders, bills, payroll reports, etc. Digital filing is recommended.

Verification of Balances – entering transactions into a bookkeeping software isn't enough to maintain accurate bookkeeping. The balances in the S Corps books must be verified on a periodic basis to determine accuracy.

Many business owners feel as though bookkeeping should be easy enough for them to handle, but usually find themselves overwhelmed by the task, or they create messes of their books. These delays can be costly to a business in missed opportunities, paying professionals to clean-up the mess, and late tax filings.

Takeaway: Bookkeeping isn't optional. If you aren't a bookkeeping pro, hire someone who is so that you can focus on what you do best.

Payroll

Payroll compliance, like bookkeeping, seems like something that should be easy for most people to handle. The reality is that payroll compliance is one of the most common ways a business ends up in hot water with the IRS, state, and local authorities. S Corps with at least one shareholder who provides services to the S Corp must run payroll. This payroll should be run at least monthly to show compliance with reasonable compensation requirements.

Takeaway: Don't mess with payroll on your own. We recommend a third-party payroll processor.

Tax Filings

S Corporations require annual 1120S & State Tax Returns to be filed on a timely basis. They are due March 15th each year or with a timely filed extension until September 15th. Failure to file these returns on time comes with hefty penalties.

Takeaway: Make your S Corp tax filings a priority each year.

Accurate & timely bookkeeping with proper payroll compliance creates the ability for S Corps to file timely and accurate tax returns.

Retirement Savings & Benefit Options

S Corporations can establish the same retirement vehicles as other entity types, however being an S Corporation shareholder-employee may result in lesser available profit- sharing contributions. This is because contributions are based on W-2 wages. Small wages = small profit sharing.

Health benefits are a big topic for many S Corporation shareholders. S Corp shareholders are not eligible to participate in an S Corporation's pre-tax health plan or some health reimbursement plans. The health insurance for an S Corporation shareholder is deductible provided the S Corp takes the proper steps to report the health insurance premiums on the shareholder's W-2. This is another compliance piece that many S Corporations miss.

Takeaway: Take into consideration your retirement goals and health benefit needs before electing to be an S Corporation shareholder.

Board Meetings & Corporate Minutes

While board meetings and corporate minutes are not a requirement of S Corporations, they are part of the best practices that can be of assistance in the event of legal action, taxing authority audits, etc.

It is recommended that board meetings be held at least annually, and corporation binders be updated accordingly.

S Corp Compliance Requirements Summary

Phew. That was a lot, right? I feel like it was, so here is your compliance checklist:

Compliance Checklist

1. Establish and maintain reasonable shareholder compensation.
2. Make careful and diligent decisions in distributing cash and property to shareholders.
3. Establish and maintain an accountable reimbursement plan for all employees.
4. Establish and maintain basis schedules for all shareholders.
5. Establish and maintain proper loan agreements for all loans between the S Corp and shareholders.
6. Establish and maintain bookkeeping on at least a monthly basis.
7. Establish and maintain payroll compliance at a minimum frequency of monthly.

8. File annual tax returns timely and accurately.
9. Establish and maintain retirement and benefit programs with required compliance for S Corporation shareholders.
10. Bonus: Establish and maintain a corporate binder with annual board meetings and corporate minutes.

Okay – do you feel like you can handle all of that? Okay. Let's talk tax savings.

Will An S Corp Save YOU Taxes?

The "tax savings" from S Corps comes from a reduction in self-employment or FICA/Medicare taxes. Historically these savings have been inflated by shareholders improperly taking very low salaries for decades. These low salaries can create a whole host of long-range financial wellness issues. Also, with the invention of the Qualified Business Income Deduction

(QBI), we are finding that less and less small businesses benefit tax-wise from forming S Corporations.

So, the big question:

Can S Corporations help save business owners taxes? Yes. Does that mean an S Corporation will save YOU taxes? That depends.

Let's look at a couple examples. To keep things simple, in both scenarios the taxpayer is single and uses the standard deduction and has no other taxable income or deductions.

Example #1:

Our veterinarian friend from above has a single member LLC, VetCo, LLC, which provides in-home euthanasia and end of life services in the Denver Metro area. They currently file the business taxes as a Sch C. They would be the only employee, and they work full-time. The business nets $100k a year and using the many hats approach results in a reasonable salary of $80k. Payroll taxes on the $80k are $12k and additional bookkeeping, payroll filing and tax professional costs of $4k/yr. Their effective tax rate is 15%.

Let's see if an S Corp election creates tax, or more importantly, cash savings:

	Sch C	S Corp
Wages	-	$80,000
VetCo, LLC	$100,000	7,000
Total Income	100,000	87,000
½ Self-Employment Taxes	7,065	-
Total Adjustments	7,065	-
Adjusted Gross Income	92,935	87,000
Standard Deduction	12,500	12,500
QBI Deduction	16,000	1,400
Total Deductions	28,500	13,900
Taxable Income	64,435	73,100
Federal Taxes @ 15%	9,665	10,965
Self-Employment Taxes	14,125	-
Total Taxes	23,790	10,965
Add'l Compliance Costs:		
Payroll Taxes	-	12,000
Compliance Costs	-	4,000
Total Compliance Costs	-	16,000
After Tax Compliance Costs	-	13,600
Total Taxes & Compliance Costs	23,790	24,565
Total (Cost) /Savings – S Corp		(866)

In this example, an S Corp doesn't save the client any money and likely will cost them time in compliance activities. Let's try another example.

Example #2:

Our veterinarian friend from above has a single member LLC, VetCo, LLC, and runs a veterinary practice in the Denver Metro area. They currently file the business taxes as a Sch C. They currently have 2 additional doctors and 5 support staff as employees, and they work full-time.

The business nets $250k a year and using the many hats approach results in a reasonable salary of $110k. Payroll taxes on the $110k are $17k and they already have established book-keeping, payroll compliance and a tax professional so there would be additional tax filing costs of $2k/yr for their S Corp tax returns. Their effective tax rate is 25%.

Let's see if an S Corp election creates tax, or more importantly, cash savings:

	Sch C	S Corp
Wages	$-	$110,000
VetCo, LLC	250,000	129,500
Total Income	250,000	239,500
½ Self-Employment Taxes	12,200	-
Total Adjustments	12,200	-
Adjusted Gross Income	237,800	239,500
Standard Deduction	12,500	12,500
QBI Deduction	-	-
Total Deductions	12,500	12,500
Taxable Income	225,300	227,000
Federal Taxes @ 25%	56,325	56,750
Self-Employment Taxes	24,680	-
Total Taxes	81,005	56,750
Add'l Compliance Costs:		
Payroll Taxes	-	17,000
Compliance Costs	-	2,000
Total Compliance Costs	-	19,000
After Tax Compliance Costs	-	14,250
Total Taxes & Compliance Costs	81,005	71,000
Total (Cost)/Savings – S Corp		10,005

In this example there is tax savings of an amount that likely would have the client choosing to make an S Election and take on the compliance activities necessary to maintain an S Corporation.

The bottom line is that S Corporations aren't the magical, tax saving unicorn that they are sold to be and making the decision to establish one isn't a 'one size fits all' solution. Look before you leap.

Tax Tip

Print off the Compliance Checklist
and complete the items.

Talk to your tax advisor to thoroughly
understand if an S Corporation
structure is right for your business.

About the Author
Jamie E. O'Kane, CPA, CTC

Jamie E. O'Kane, CPA, CTC is owner of the Colorado-based CPA firm Abundant Beans Tax & Accounting, and the host of *The Abundant Beans Podcast.*

Abundant Beans Tax & Accounting provides goal-based & proactive tax strategy, tax compliance, and consulting services that make a positive impact on their client' ability to build sustainable businesses. Their niche is women-owned veterinary and dental practices.

Women practice owners are changing the game in their industries, and nothing fires up the team at Abundant Beans Tax & Accounting more than helping them do it.

Company: Abundant Beans Tax & Accounting

Website: www.abundantbeans.com

To learn more about Jamie and the team at Abundant Beans Tax & Accounting, please visit www.abundantbeans.com.

MISTAKE #5: MISCLASSIFYING WORKER

BY SHAWN HARJU

Is Hiring Multiple Independent Contractors Really a Better Option than Hiring Employees?

A common misconception of small business owners is that it will be easier and less expensive to hire independent contractors rather than employees. An ever-expanding gig economy, along with a growing number of regulations protecting employees, lends to this reasoning by business owners.

Independent Contractors versus Employees

Increasingly, individuals in search of more flexibility are not necessarily looking for the typical employment situation and as a result, are open to the idea of being an independent contractor. Hiring an independent contractor is viewed as a business-to-business relationship governed by whatever contract the parties decide to enter into rather than the myriad of employment laws imposing certain duties on employers as it relates to their employees. Generally speaking, a business is not required (or expected) to provide certain benefits such as health insurance, pension or retirement, life insurance, disability, paid time off (vacation or sick leave) or bonuses to an independent contractor. Such benefits are not only expected, but sometimes required, in a typical employer- employee relationship.*

A business entering into a contract with an independent contractor cannot only define and plan for its risks and costs related to that particular relationship but can shift some of those risks and costs to the independent contractor. For example, by the very nature of the independent contractor relationship, the business is not required to withhold or pay any federal taxes related to the services provided by the independent contractor. It is solely the responsibility of the independent contractor to pay federal taxes on the compensation it receives. The business can also require the independent contractor to carry insurance of varying types and amounts that will protect the business in the instance of a breach of contract by the independent contractor. No such protection is available to the business in the relationship with its employee.

While an employer may have a written employment contract with an employee, many of the terms of that agreement are defined and governed by federal, state, and (sometimes) local law, leaving the business little or no ability to control its costs or shift the related risks to the employee. Employers are also required to pay and withhold income, social security, Medicare and unemployment taxes, as well as premiums for workers' compensation insurance. Depending on business size and location (among other things), an employer may also be required to provide certain benefits such as health insurance to its employees.

Classification of Independent Contractors

A business focusing solely on such risks and costs tends to lose sight of the costly consequences of misclassifying someone as an independent contractor rather than an employee. Such misclassification occurs when a business identifies someone performing work for them as an independent contractor, but the nature of the relationship is akin to that of an employer and an employee. If it is determined by a governing agency, i.e., IRS, state agency governing unemployment or workers' compensation, that an individual should have been classified as an employee, the business which misclassified that person as an independent contractor may not only be required to pay the taxes and premiums that would have been otherwise owed but significant interest and penalties. The misclassification of one such independent contractor may also result in subjecting the business to an audit that could lead to additional penalties if it is discovered that multiple parties were misclassified as independent contractors.

Governing agencies such as the IRS and state agencies governing unemployment and workers' compensation use multi-factor tests to determine whether an individual qualifies as an independent contractor or an employee. Assuming that the business can demonstrate that its relationship with that particular individual meets the multi- factor tests, it will be exempt from the legal requirements (including payment of various taxes and premiums) applicable to the employer-employee relationship. To avoid the costly consequences of misclassifying someone as an independent contractor, it is advisable to first determine whether your relationship with that person will satisfy the applicable multi-factor tests. Regardless of which multi-factor test applies, it is necessary to look at the entirety of your relationship with the person providing services to your business and to document each factor you use to determine the nature of the relationship.

Classification by the Internal Revenue Service

The primary consideration of the IRS' multi-factor test is the degree of control and independence that exists in your relationship with the individual providing services. The information that demonstrates the degree of control and independence for the IRS' purposes falls into the following three (3) categories:

1. **Behavioral.** Whether the business controls or has the right to control what the individual does and how the person does his job.
2. **Financial.** Does the business control the business aspects of the individual's work such as how he is paid, whether he is reimbursed for his expenses, who provides the tools and supplies to perform the work?
3. **Type of Relationship.** Do the parties have a written contract, or will the individual receive employee benefits such as a pension plan, insurance, or paid time off? How long will the relationship last? Is the work being performed a key aspect of your business?

Not one of these factors on its own will determine whether the individual is an independent contractor. Additionally, which factors are relevant will vary depending on the particular situation. It is also important to note that simply having a written contract in place does not guarantee the existence of an independent contractor relationship, particularly if an examination of the actual relationship demonstrates the existence of an employer-employee relationship.

For those businesses which want to be absolutely sure of their determination, they can submit to the IRS a Form SS-8 that requests a determination from the IRS. While this can take at least six (6) months, businesses who are regularly hiring the same type of workers may benefit from having this determination in hand. Form SS-8 can be submitted by the entity hiring the independent contractor or by the party being hired.

No matter the determination you make, it is extremely important to consistently treat that individual in the same way, i.e., if you determine to treat someone as an independent contractor, do not take any actions that may result in them being viewed as an employee. As long as you are consistent in your treatment of such individuals and have a reasonable basis for treating them as an independent contractor, you may be relieved from paying unemployment taxes for those individuals. Suddenly classifying someone as an independent contractor who has been classified as an employee for an extended timeframe may not entitle you to such relief.

Once you have determined that the person you are hiring will be in the capacity of an independent contractor, you must have them complete a Form W-9, which will provide you with their correct name and taxpayer identification number. The Form W-9 should be kept in your records for at least four (4) years. You must also file, annually, a Form 1099-NEC with the IRS to report any payments of nonemployee compensation you make to the independent contractor in excess of $600 for that particular year. A copy of Form 1099-NEC must also be provided to the independent contractor.

To the extent that your independent contractors have their own employees and/or independent contractors, they need to be aware of their tax responsibilities. You want to ensure that they are contractually required to fulfill those responsibilities so as not to expose you to liability for them.

State Classification

Even if you have determined that the person you are hiring qualifies as an independent contractor pursuant to the IRS test, it is important to confirm that he or she also qualifies pursuant to the applicable tests of other agencies such as state agencies that regulate unemployment and workers' compensation. Since the tests may not be identical to those of the IRS, failure to do so can lead to you paying additional back taxes and premiums to state agencies. Individual state agencies may also have their own tests, so it is important to understand the requirements of each of those agencies so as not to find yourself paying unexpected taxes and/or premiums and the related penalties and interest.

Similar to the IRS, state agencies typically have at least one multi-factor test. They may even have different tests for different industries. For example, Washington state implements one test as to those in the construction and electrical industry and another as to all other industries. Notably, a general contractor who does not ensure that its subcontractors and their respective sub-subcontractors are appropriately classified as independent contractors can find itself paying its subcontractors' workers' compensation premiums.

Since a Form 1099 is a federal form, it does not necessarily have any bearing on whether a party is considered an independent contractor under state law. And, just as with the IRS multi-factor test, the existence of a written agreement may not guarantee the existence of an independent contractor relationship. The applicable law of the state in which the proposed independent contractor resides will need to be examined to determine the relevance of these items in determining whether the person is, in fact, an independent contractor or an employee.

It is also important to note that some states have instituted certain protections for independent contractors similar to those provided to employees. For example, Washington state has only very narrow exemptions related to the payment of workers' compensation premiums for independent contractors. So, although you may not be required to pay unemployment taxes for an independent contractor, you may still find yourself paying workers' compensation premiums.

Summary

As a small business owner, the tendency can be to take the route that, on the surface appears to be the easiest and less expensive, i.e., not paying the taxes and other amounts related to hiring employees. However, taking that route when it comes to misclassifying your employees as independent contractors can lead to significant unexpected costs. Taking the time to analyze the applicable federal and state tests, determining whether your classifications are accurate, and acting accordingly are likely much less costly in the long run.

Tax Tip

Misclassifying your employees as independent contractors can be costly.

Make sure you complete the tests in this chapter so you stay in compliance with federal and state laws.

About the Author
Shawn K. Harju

I am a Nantucket island native but have spent most of my life in the Pacific Northwest. My favorite part of practicing law is getting to know my clients and their businesses and helping them be proactive and practical in their risk management and problem-solving, After earning my degree at the University of Pittsburgh, I graduated from Seattle University's School of Law.

I started Chrysalis Solutions in late 2020 to follow my desire to provide easily accessible legal and business resources to small business owners.

Company: Chrysalis Solutions PLLC

Website: www.chrysalissolutionspllc.com

Email: shawn@chrysalissolutionspllc.com

Phone: 253-517-3622

MISTAKE #6: NOT HAVING PROPER BOOKKEEPING

BY LILY TRAN, EA, CTC

There is no question that bad bookkeeping practices can lead to big trouble with the IRS, with your bank or finance lender, and with your tax professional. And studies have shown that poor bookkeeping practices translate to poor business management and operations, and a higher incidence of business failure. Bookkeeping covers many different facets of your business finances, so we will explore some of the most common mistakes entrepreneurs make in this area. Thankfully, many of the mistakes made in bookkeeping are easy to find and fix.

1. Commingling Personal & Business Funds

This is one of the biggest issues small business owners have because they don't realize how important it is to keep business money separate from personal money. It can be understandable because they might think that it shouldn't matter because it's all going to the same place at the end of the day—but the IRS doesn't see it this way. To ensure you don't commingle funds, keep a separate bank account and separate credit cards for personal and business transactions.

. . .

2. Failure to Track All Your Expenses

Most small business owners try to track the money they spend, but they might forget some expenses when they get busy, or not know what expenses are actually tax deductible so they decide in the moment what they think is worth tracking. This is a mistake because some unexpected expenses are tax deductible. Track all expenses, and if you're unsure, you can ask your tax advisor for more guidance on your specific needs.

3. Not Having Accounting Software

Gone are the days of shoe boxes and faded receipts. Now is the time to purchase and use accounting software for your small business, whether you are just starting out or have been operating for some time. What used to take a lot of time, energy, and money can now be done quickly and easily with the click of a few buttons. Accounting and bookkeeping software enables you to connect your bank and credit card accounts capturing all transactions into the software system and allows you to then properly designate each transaction to the right business category. After you have classified all payments and deposits, it's critical you reconcile your accounts. Bookkeeping programs help you save time because the transactions are automatically imported and organized for you. Whether you hire a bookkeeper or manage your books on your own, it's vital you have your tax professional thoroughly review your file. After learning the software program, most entrepreneurs also use the reporting functions to generate profit & loss statements, balance sheets, and cash flow for their business over a set period of time to help make revenue, sales, operations, or growth goals.

. . .

4. Failure to Save Receipts

Oftentimes, small business owners believe that their credit card or debit card statements are good enough to show their expenses because it has the date, the amount, and the store. Let's say you spend $100 at a superstore that sells many different products, like hardware supplies and liquor and groceries and paint, how does the IRS know what you actually spent it on? Keep every receipt that shows a business expense and write on the receipt what was purchased, for what reason, the date and amount (since receipts fade or smudge so quickly), and if it is a meal or business meeting, who you were with and what you discussed. You might think it's a lot of work to record this information on every purchase but in an audit, the IRS will reject receipts that don't meet the criteria for qualified expenses.

5. Not Filing Tax Returns on Time

Small business owners have so much to manage, keeping track of dates and deadlines often slip their mind. If the deadline is to cancel a streaming subscription, the consequence is small. If the deadline is to pay taxes, the consequences could be very significant. The IRS does not have any leeway for small business owners who delay filing and miss paying their taxes on time and there are hefty penalties for those not completing those tasks on time.

6. Being Unprepared Means You Pay More

The more unorganized you are, the more money you will pay to your tax professional because they will charge you to organize your financial records, catalog all your receipts and transactions, and track down documents you might have misplaced or lost. To make the most of your time with your tax professional and pay the least amount possible, know what they need to help you, like having your annual revenue and expenses itemized and totaled, receipts sorted and labeled, and all documentation available.

7. Not Keeping Documents Long Enough

Many small business owners are happy to file their taxes and then not deal with the tax return anymore, but the IRS has rules around how long one must keep their tax records and receipts. Three years is sufficient in most cases, but some cases call for documents to be stored and available for seven years. Have the paper copies and digital copies stored separately, and label them so you know where to find them should the IRS decide to audit your business.

8. Not Billing Clients on a Set Schedule

There are many reasons why invoices or payments might not go out on time, but erratic invoicing to your clients makes proper bookkeeping nearly impossible. Plus, when bills go out at various times, in an unpredictable manner, clients don't pay in a timely manner because the expectation of being on time is not modeled for them. Set and stick to a billing schedule for each client, and track when invoices will go out to them, the due date of the invoice, and a 'past due' date you either send a reminder or you give your client a call to see if everything is alright.

9. Not Checking Bank Accounts Regularly

Mistakes are made, and it is our responsibility to make sure that any mistakes in our accounts are fixed quickly and correctly. There may be false charges on a credit card, or a refund that was never processed, or a discount that wasn't honored, and we will never know if we don't reconcile our bank accounts. The recommendation is once a month, look at your bank statements, credit card statements, and other payment systems and make sure the money you expect to be there is there, the money you paid out is gone, and there are no surprises. If you look at your documents every few months, you might think things look fine, but since we don't remember the details of all transactions, it's easy to miss something amiss.

10. You Have Cash Flow Problems

With lax bookkeeping practices, you will most certainly experience cash flow challenges, and often it comes in the form of overdrawn charges on your bank accounts because you didn't have enough funds to cover a charge, or late payments because you missed a deadline. Having strong bookkeeping practices in place will mean your money in and money out can be more in flow, having a predictable and dependable schedule.

Tax Tip

Good bookkeeping is a must.
Implement good tracking habits and
organize your documents so you can
find what you need if required.

Stay on top of updating your records
regularly so you track all your income
and business expenses.

About the Author
Lily Tran, EA, CTC, NTPI Fellow

 Lily is the Founder of TaxUSign®—providing virtual tax help for whatever life throws at you™. Lily is part of an elite group of tax professionals licensed by the IRS as an Enrolled Agent (EA), a federal program authorizing her to represent taxpayers before the IRS when it comes to audits, collections, and appeals. She's a Certified Tax Coach specializing in tax planning strategies, as well as an NTPI Fellow.

Lily is a graduate of the University of Washington, and has nearly two decades of experience in accounting, tax, consulting, and advisory services for small business owners and corporations. She is a member of the National Association of Enrolled Agents, past Director of Washington State of Enrolled Agents, and past Treasurer of Washington State Tax Consultants. She has been featured in Forbes, Bloomberg Tax and Accounting, SUCCESS Magazine, and the Journal of Accountancy. She is also a co-author on a children's story book called *Meet the Spunkiez Heroes*™, with her son, and enjoys living with her family the Pacific Northwest.

Company: TaxUSign

Website: https://www.taxusign.com

If you would like a consultation, please book a session on the TaxUSign website.

MISTAKE #7: CLAIMING TOO MANY BUSINESS EXPENSES

BY HARLEY SHERMAN, CPA

Expensing for Income Taxes

The recognition of a business expense in the accounting records and tax returns of a business is not as clear as one might think. Also, what is deductible in the accounting records might not be deductible for income tax purposes. Expense accounting for financial statement purposes, typically follows Generally Accepted Accounting Principles. However, reporting expense deductions on an income tax return follows the Internal Revenue Code.

The Internal Revenue Code (Chapter 26, Section 162), allows as a deduction 'all the ordinary and necessary expenses paid or incurred during the taxable year in carrying on any trade or business.' The section continues providing examples and exceptions. For our purposes, we will stick to the generality of the Code's definition.

Ordinary and Necessary

To be ordinary, an expense must be commonplace for a particular industry or practice. To be necessary, the specific business must have and use the particular item for the purposes of providing the goods and or services it provides. For example, it is common for an auto repair shop to have tools to change oil as well as a hoist to pull an engine.

However, if the repair shop only does oil changes, then the hoist would not be necessary.

Buried in the ordinary and necessary terminology is that the cost must be reasonable. For a home-based business with minimal printing needs, a printer for a few hundred dollars would probably serve the need. However, spending a few thousand dollars on an industrial printer is not reasonable and upon audit could be disallowed.

Cash or Accrued Expense

Cash-basis taxpayers report and take the expense deduction in the year the expense was paid. Accrual-basis taxpayers report and take the expense deduction in the year the benefit was received. For example, a business pays a retainer of $1,200.00 to an attorney for six months of service starting December. On a cash-basis, the business would get a $1,200.00 expense in that year. If the business was on the accrual-basis, there would be a $200.00 expense in the first year (one month of service) and the balance would be expensed in the second year.

There are certain rules specifying when an entity can be on the cash-basis or when it must use the accrual-basis. Also, once a method is selected, a business cannot switch between the two each year. So, before making the decision, it is wise to 1) determine if the accrual method is required; and 2) if the accrual method is not required, think through the implications of each choice.

Period Expense or Capital Expenditure

A Period Expense is an expenditure that is expected to benefit only the current year and is of relatively low cost. A Capital Expenditure is an expenditure when the benefit is expected to last at least one year and cost a significant amount of money. Buying a stapler for $15.00, one would assume the stapler would last longer than one year. However, the cost is not significant and would be treated as a period expense.

Certain software can cost thousands of dollars, leading one to think it would be a Capital Expenditure. However, if the software is only good for one year (like tax prep software), then it would be a Period Expense.

Under current IRS rules, an election can be made to allow the expense (rather than capitalization) of an expenditure costing $2500.00 or less. This is optional. A business can set its own threshold, but again it must be reasonable. If the annual revenue for a business is $100,000.00 then choosing a threshold of $10,000.00 is not reasonable.

Be sure to have a documented policy on the capitalization of expenditures. This should include Period vs Capital, thresholds, and depreciation methods.

Depreciation methods for income taxes do differ between financial accounting and income tax. For financial accounting, there are various methods. The key is reasonable and consistent. For income tax purposes, the IRS requires certain methods.

Expenditures Never Deductible

Even though a business incurs an expense it may not be deductible on the income tax return. One example of this is entertainment. Under current tax law, entertainment is no longer a deductible expense. For most small businesses (non-C Corp), charitable donations are also not deductible, but can be reported on a personal tax return.

. . .

Special Situations

There are some special situations, under the accrual basis, when an expense is incurred but cannot be taken until paid. One common example is when the owner loans money to the business. Based on the loan document, a certain amount of interest is computed on the loan balance. The loans are typically 'demand loans', meaning the loan does not get paid back until the lender demands it. Regardless, interest expense is still building, and the interest expense is reported in the accounting records.

However, the expense cannot be deducted on the income tax return until the interest is paid.

The Home Office Deduction for the business owner working out of the personal residence offers a few options. Before getting to those options, the office must be a space dedicated to the exclusive purpose of conducting business. Thus, the space of the dining room table would not be allowed as it is not for the specific use of the business. A dedicated room could qualify for the deduction. The risk here is in the amount of use. If the office is used 1 hour per week but the taxpayer claims a deduction for the full year, this could be an audit issue.

Assuming the home office does qualify, there are two methods of determining the deduction. The first is the Safe Harbor. This is determined by multiplying the square footage of the office by $5.00. This is up to office space of 300 square feet. Thus, a maximum of $1,500.00 would be allowed as a deduction. Not only is this quick and easy, but it also allows the homeowner to apply mortgage interest and property taxes fully to potentially itemizing deductions on Schedule A of the 1040 tax return.

The second option is the actual expense. This option requires the allocation of expenses between the office space and the whole house. One would need the square footage of the office as well as the whole house. In this case, mortgage interest, property tax, utilities, maintenance, etc. are allocated between the office space and the rest of the house. There would also be the requirement of depreciation of the value of the office space relative to the value of the house. There is no square footage limitation using this method. If a business owner had a house measuring 2,500 square feet and used 400 square feet as office, then 16% of the expenses would be allocated as office deductions. Expenses specifically related to the office would be 100% deductible as home office. Besides being time consuming, another downside of this method is the capital gain exclusion on the sale of personal residence is diminished.

Automobile mileage is another special situation. The IRS requires a written record of the mileage reported for business deduction. This could be a handwritten log, documented calendar, or mileage app. There is no standard mileage allowance. The expense is the miles multiplied by the rate per mile in the IRS website (www.irs.gov).

Details that need reporting are total miles for the year, commuting miles, and business miles. Commuting miles are those miles driven from your home to your place of business or to your first stop for business. If the owner uses a home office, then any business-related miles from home are reported as business miles.

Hobby Rules

Some businesses are really a hobby. There are several factors that go into this determination. The primary factor is whether the activity is for profit or for fun. Assuming it is for profit, at some point the IRS may ask for evidence of the business purpose.

Generally, the IRS will accept an activity as profit- motivated if there is profit in three of the past five years. If there is no profit and the owner cannot substantiate, then the IRS will probably reclassify the activity as a hobby. In the case of a hobby, the income is taxable, but the expenses are taken on Schedule A as an itemized deduction.

Documentation

The key to taking an expenditure as a tax deduction is having supporting documentation. It's not enough to say, "I had this expense last year, just use that" or "My mileage is the same as last year." These are things the IRS looks for. The best documentation is a signed receipt or the mileage log. In the past several years, the IRS has disallowed the use of a checkbook register or a canceled check. One might think, the canceled check proves something was purchased. However, it does not prove what was purchased and the business purpose.

Many receipts are printed on paper where the ink fades or smudges and makes it unreadable. It is a wise idea to do one or more of the following:

1. Scan a copy to your accounting software
2. Scan a copy, store on computer and the cloud
3. Use a pen to note the date, amount, items, and place of purchase, and keep it in a safe place

Meals require special documentation. The date of the meal, the person met with, and the business purpose must be documented. The meal must be immediately before or after the meeting. Going to dinner with your business partner or client and asking, 'How's business?' is not enough.

What to do when the records no longer exist? All is not lost. For those who do not have the support, the Cohen Rule allows a taxpayer to use reasonable estimates for expenses provided there is some factual basis for the deduction.

• • •

Fallacies

Setting aside the Cohen Rule, the IRS takes the stance on expense deductions; "if there is no documentation the expense is disallowed." Therefore, the following will probably not work:

1. It is what I have always done
2. My friend is in a similar business, and this is what he/she does
3. I flew to Hawaii and tried knocking on doors to get business meetings
4. I drove about 10,000 miles
5. Isn't there a standard expense total I can take?

Audit Risk

For the purposes of this chapter, there are two types of audit risk: 'under-reporting' and 'over-reporting' of expenses. I imagine I am getting odd looks regarding under-reporting of expenses. Like, why would anyone do that? Fair question. The obvious result of under-reporting expenses is to increase reported income. Many that do this do so because showing a higher income helps in getting a mortgage or other debt financing. Now there are ways to do such things within the IRS Code. One way is to use the tax depreciation method rather than Section 179 or Bonus Depreciation.

Likewise, over-reporting expenses is an audit risk as well. We have talked at length about this above. There are two additional items to add though. One is rebates. A rebate is money back on a purchase. Sometimes the rebates are in the form of a check and the owner just goes to the bank and cashes the check; it never gets reported in the financial records or income tax returns. Another case would be when something is returned for a refund or a credit. In these cases, the expense is not offset by the refund.

Remember, it is the taxpayer that signs the tax return indicating that the information being reported in the tax return is true and accurate to the best of the taxpayer's knowledge. If the taxpayer provides documentation of some sort to the preparer and the preparer relies on that information, the taxpayer is probably going to face some type of IRS action. While preparers are required to do a certain amount of due diligence, they are not required to detect fraud or prove everything is 100%.

On the flipside, the taxpayer must make sure the preparer reported what actually occurred. If the tax return shows a home office deduction, but there was no home office, this needs correcting.

As a final note, be sure to get an engagement letter and that the tax preparer signs the tax return and indicates the preparer ID number. The engagement letter protects the payer and preparer and indicates the responsibilities of both. If the preparer does not sign the return, the taxpayer will be hard pressed to prove who prepared and filed the return.

Tax Tip

When it comes to your tax filing, both over-reporting and under-reporting can lead to serious issues with the IRS.

Ensure you have documentation for everything you are claiming.

About the Author
Harley M. Sherman, CPA

 Harley has over 20 years of experience in personal and business income tax, small business start-up activities, and accounting. He has been responsible for servicing clients in the medical, food service, real estate, construction, and cannabis industries. Harley began working with the cannabis industry in the spring of 2016 when he started his own firm. His focus is on educating his clients so they can make informed decisions.

Harley is a 1985 graduate of Central Michigan University where he received his Bachelor of Science degree; in 1994, he earned his Masters of Science in Professional Accountancy from Walsh College. Harley is an Adjunct Professor of Accounting and Income Tax at Oakland Community College. In his spare time, Harley enjoys cooking, reading about military history, and refinishing wood furniture. A life-long resident of Southeast Michigan, he lives in Oak Park with his family, three dogs and a cat.

Company: Harley M. Sherman, CPA, Inc

Website: www.hmshermancpa.com

Email: harley@hmshermancpa.com

Phone: 586-286-0915

MISTAKE #8: MILEAGE ROUNDING OR MISSING MILEAGE

BY ELLIE NAVA-JONES, EA, MLS

It Costs Money Because it Saves Money: Transportation Expenses

In the 1987 film *Moonstruck,* the father, Cosmo Castorini, is a plumber providing a quote to a couple whose plumbing is gray and flaking. The wife balks at the number--it is $10,000 in 1987 dollars (just under $24,000 in 2021 dollars) --to which Cosmo replies: "It costs money. It costs money because it saves money."

At first blush, it appears that Cosmo is scamming the couple, but the maxim isn't any less true. Although the initial investment in copper plumbing is extensive, it saves them money due to the longevity of the materials and the workmanship. When it comes to running a business, putting money into services such as bookkeepers, tax professionals, and their apps, may appear as an excessive outlay of funds, a dip in the cash flow, but it will inevitably save money. (And in my limited knowledge, copper plumbing is a superior product).

Good bookkeeping saves money- after all, it is a deduction as a professional fee. Thorough and accurate tracking of income and expenses ensures all available deductions and other tax write- offs are included, and reduces the risk of not having those claims at all, like if receipts are crammed into shoeboxes, or if a taxpayer relies on memories, or if they say, "the deduction is the same as last year." And good bookkeeping saves on time as taxes are often prepared more efficiently and with less emails or phone calls with your preparer (and some firms may offer a small discount on a return if the books are organized).

Finally, good bookkeeping can protect you during an IRS or state tax examination. At last, this potential sales pitch and excessively long prologue, arrives at its thesis statement: without effective bookkeeping, taxpayers historically rely on round numbers and repeat numbers which sends up red flags within the IRS computers. A particular area in which the IRS concentrates is mileage. The purpose of this section is to discuss how the IRS scores a return for examination and to discuss the complex rules of mileage, with an eye toward easing the bookkeeping burden.

How IRS Scores a Return

No one is quite sure of the magic formula that the IRS uses when determining which taxpayers will be audited. However, one thing that tax professionals know is that the IRS uses computers to score returns and to generate something called a Discriminant Function System, or DIF, score. The IRS does not share what goes into the DIF score, only that the returns with the highest DIF score are then reviewed by personnel and then they decide to send out an audit examination request. This sort of letter means that the IRS wants to examine how you, the taxpayer, arrived at your numbers that you reported as income and expenses.

A few areas for business owners that crop up frequently on audit examination requests are travel and mileage deductions. The IRS has enough information in most fields to determine how much travel and mileage is ordinary and necessary. The

IRS derives its regulations from the US Tax code and, in Chapter 26, Section 162, we find the watch words: "There shall be allowed as a deduction all the ordinary and necessary expenses paid or incurred during the taxable year in carrying on any trade or business."

Ordinary and necessary. Are these expenses typical in this field? Is a trip to Costa Rica a necessary and ordinary expense for a truck driver? Is a $25,000 mileage expense ordinary and necessary for a realtor? If the IRS is receiving 200 million tax returns, then they can take the totals and create databases to determine what is typical in any given field. Is it unusual for a roofing contractor in the greater Cincinnati area to drive more than 12,000 miles? Are these ordinary and necessary?

In addition to outrageous and unusual numbers, the IRS will ask questions about round numbers and mileage. If the IRS receives a Schedule C where every number ends with 00, they will score this return higher. It's because it most likely indicates that the taxpayer did not keep an accurate and complete set of records.

And an easy area where taxpayers do not often keep complete and accurate records? Mileage. Let's explore this deduction.

Transportation: Mileage or Actual Expenses

Taxpayers are allowed a deduction for the business use of their vehicle. For the purposes of this chapter, we will be talking about cars, small SUVs, and trucks. There are different rules for motorcycles and large trucks over 6,000 pounds.

A taxpayer has two methods from which to choose when taking a deduction for business use of a vehicle. They can take actual expenses which is the total of the gas, oil changes, repairs, tires, registration, insurance, and depreciation. This must be prorated by the business use of the car. If the taxpayer uses the car for business 50% of the time, then they will take

50% of those actual expenses. They must also depreciate the car which is the annual reduction in the value of property.

Or a taxpayer can elect to take mileage, which is a rate set annually by the IRS for business use of a vehicle. Mileage includes everything in actual expenses, all rolled up in one amount. For the tax year, 2021 mileage expense is 0.56 cents a mile. If a taxpayer drove 5,000 business miles in 2021, the 5,000 would be multiplied by 0.56 for a deduction of $2,800 (sometimes it is a rounded number but if most entries are rounded, a red flag is raised).

If a taxpayer pays parking or tolls, those are not included in either the actual or mileage expense. These are separate expenses and should be reported in Other Expenses (and some tax professionals say it goes into Travel). Mileage can vary based on the reason, such as charity or medical.

How would you decide to take mileage or actual expense? Under the tax code, you want to take the one that will give you a better deduction. If you meet with a CPA or an Enrolled Agent (EA), or another tax professional, they will often compare an actual deduction vs mileage and will advocate for the one that reduces your tax liability the most.

Mileage is often the most beneficial deduction as everything is rolled up into it and the mileage rate is adjusted every year. The first year you use a car for business, however, is the most crucial.

- If you use the actual expenses method for the first year you use a vehicle for a business, you must use actual expenses for five years (the useful life of a vehicle)
- If you use the mileage expenses for the first year you use a vehicle for a business, you can switch between actual and mileage.

As you can see, mileage starts off with a bigger benefit. The flexibility to select the method with the highest deduction is useful, especially as income fluctuates. But business use of a car is very specific.

Let's define some key terms before we begin.

Home: The place where you reside. Traveling between home and the main place of work is considered commuting. For example, Amber drives Monday through Friday from her home to her office. This is a commute and does not count toward an automobile related deduction.

Regular or main job: The primary place of business. If you have more than one job, you need to decide which one is your main job by confirming which one you spend the most time at during a period of time, the amount of work you do at each, and the income you earn from each.

Temporary work location: A place where you are temporarily assigned. Could be for a job location (ex: a roofer in a new development installing roofs on all the new homes). A temporary job location is a job that will last less than one year. Unless you have a regular place of business, you can only deduct your transportation expenses to a temporary work location outside of your city.

Second job: If you regularly work at two or more places, whether for the same employer or not, you can deduct transportation expenses of getting from one workplace to another. You can't deduct expenses from your home to the second job if it is a day off from your main job.

(Tip: If you are an employee, you cannot deduct mileage between a first job and second job on your federal return anymore. Under the Tax Cuts and Jobs Act (TCJA), the unreimbursed employee expenses have been suspended until 2026. However, some states, such as California and New York, do not follow all the TCJA and you may be able to get a deduction on your state return.)

If you do a lot of driving as an employee, you might want to talk to your employer about an accountable plan. For example, if you drive between oil rigs owned by the same company in your car, you would want to request mileage reimbursement. If it's in a company car, then it does not apply to your personal returns.

Mileage and commuting are one of the more difficult tax concepts to fully grasp. The diagram shows how easy it is to confuse a drive that counts for transportation expense from a commute.

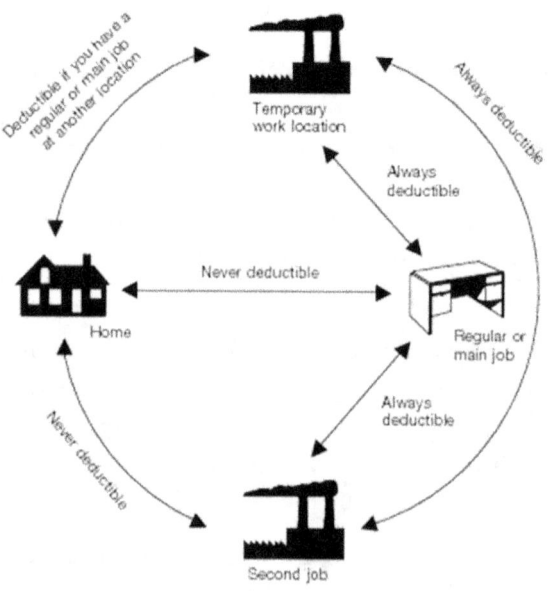

From IRS Publication 463

Here are some examples:

Example 1

Steven is a job contractor. He does massive builds on skyscrapers every year so his temporary job location can be the same place for six months or more. Because he is driving to and from the same place, he has a commute.

But let's say, Steven has to swing by an office to collect a check before going to his job site. That becomes a mileage expense.

Example 2:

Sam is a roofing contractor. He drives all around a metropolitan area, visiting various sites, picking up materials and checks, and meeting with payroll officers. He is based in Cincinnati, Ohio, which borders Kentucky, and he has clients in Kentucky as far south as Lexington (an hour's drive) and as far north as Columbus (a 90 minute drive).

His mileage is quite high.

This becomes a situation for the IRS as his mileage is higher than is normal for his field (roofing contractor).

Let's say, he has 20,500 miles. But the IRS database shows that 12,000 business mileage is typical for roofing contractors. Car & Truck Expenses, as it's called on Schedule C, is something that the IRS computers do assign a DIF score.

So then proving transportation expenses becomes the problem. Mileage falls under IRC Section 274(d) which has strict substantiation rules. (Section 274(d) also includes travel, meals and entertainment so the same strict rules apply).

For any auto expenses, it means the following:

- The amount of such expense or other item (such as miles driven)
- The time and place of the travel

- The business purpose of the trip
- The business relationship

Additionally, this log must be made contemporaneously, which means being recorded at the time it is happening. The IRS has the right to refuse any reconstructed logs or records that were created long after the driving happened. If you don't keep a detailed log of your business miles, the IRS may allow you to reconstruct a mileage log from other documents, such as calendars, diaries or appointment books. However, this reconstructed log needs to be internally consistent and credible.

This matter is consistently litigated, often all the way to US Tax Court, a special court where a taxpayer can pursue relief from a tax liability that the IRS says they are required to pay.

In Taylor vs Commission, TC Memo 2017-99, Mrs. Taylor worked full time at a hospital and ran a medical collections service as a side business. She drove all through West Virginia and various states to meet with prospective clients and to drop off brochures. Mr. Taylor ran a recycling business and for ease of use, they combined the income and expenses for both businesses on a single Schedule C when they were filing their taxes.

The IRS denied the mileage and the Taylors took it up to the Tax Court. They needed to prove $74,373 of mileage expenses. Mrs. Taylor did not keep a contemporaneous log, but she reconstructed her mileage on a spreadsheet which she presented to the Court. Her spreadsheet showed over 130,000 miles.

As the Court examined the spreadsheet, they found several inconsistencies which included:

- Odometer readings for trips in the same vehicle on different days overlapped

- Nearly all her driving consisted of long one-day round trips with an average of 900 miles a day. A judge pointed out that this would require driving nonstop at 70 mph an hour for nearly twenty-four hours
- Returning to the same area repeatedly in a week rather than combining trips

The problem with reconstructing a log is that a taxpayer can inadvertently work to make the evidence match the numbers reported on the return rather than reporting the actual numbers.

The Court did not agree with the Taylors' numbers and denied them the deduction. In addition to losing the deduction, the Taylors got hit with an accuracy related penalty, which can be anything from 10% to 20% of the tax difference.

But keeping a contemporaneous log can be arduous. Between juggling client calls, driving, ordering supplies, paying taxes and employees, and everything else that running a business requires, maintaining contemporary records can be like a straw that breaks the camel back.

On the bright side, this is where technology can save the day. Beginning in 2014, several companies began to offer mileage apps that would track your mileage for you. Many of them rely on the swipe concept--swipe left, it's business; swipe right, it's personal. (A caveat: If you have privacy concerns, they do require you to turn on your location on your cell phone).

As of writing, here are some of the more popular mileage tracking apps:

MileIQ

Free version: Up to 40 trips per month

Full version: $5.99/month, $59.99/year

Pros:	Cons:
Automatic mileage tracking: Once you flag certain routes, MileIQ will automatically detect them and classify them as expenses as you drive.	Only tracks miles: MileIQ just tracks how far you drive.
Work hours: You can set work hours when MileIQ's automatic mileage tracking is on.	It does not offer any other accounting tools.

Hurdlr

Free version: Single user, no automatic tracking

Full version: $7.99/month or $58.99/year

Pros:	Cons:
App integration with Uber, Lyft, Uber Eats, and other accounts.	
This is a full-fledged expense tracking app; mileage is just one feature.	Slow starting: It can sometimes take up to one mile before the tracking kicks in so you can lose out on some mileage.

TripLog

Free version: No automatic tracking, five vehicle limit, 40 trips per month

Full version: Premium plan is $5.99/month or $60/year, Premium+ team time tracking is $7.99/month or $80/yr.

Pros:	Cons:
Multiple vehicles and drivers on a single system: Track fleet mileage easily.	Free version excludes automatic tracking.
Many ways to track mileage: Both manual and automatic, Bluetooth connection with vehicle, compatibility with mileage tracking devices.	You have to enter mileage manually.
Photo capture for expenses: You can record receipts for expenses incurred on trips.	
As of writing, it offers a 15 day free trial.	

SherpaShare

Basic version: $5.99/month or $59.88/year

Full version: Premium starts at $10/month

Pros:	Cons:
Unlimited, automatic mileage tracking via GPS, as many trips as you make per month.	No free version.
SmartShare analytics for rideshare drivers: Track hourly revenue and profit, chat with other drivers, see a heatmap of where other drivers are active, and get recommendations.	

Everlance

Free version: Up to 30 trips per month

Premium version: $8/month or $60/year

Pros:	Cons:
Simple, clean interface: Users report that Everlance is simple and easier to use than other mileage apps.	Limited free version: 30 trips per month max on the free version is not enough for everyone.
IRS forms: Automatically generates IRS forms itemizing your mileage deductions.	If the app fails to start at the beginning of the trip, there is no automatic tracking.
Photo tracking: Snap pictures of receipts and upload them.	

If you are using Quickbooks Online, there is an option for mileage tracking via the Quickbooks app. If you are using QBO, your bookkeeper or tax professional can help you with the app. It is generally included in the monthly QBO price.

Some of these apps are better than others for different industries. If you drive for a ride sharing company, such as Lyft or Uber, SherpaShare and Hurdlr are the best options as they offer more options and can connect to whatever agency you are driving for during a shift.

A few other notes on mileage:

- Motorcycles and other two wheeled vehicles are ineligible for mileage expenses. If you drive a two wheeled vehicle for business, you must take actual expenses.
- If your company has more than five vehicles, you cannot use mileage. You must take actual expense on each vehicle.

As a business owner, you are using your vehicle to visit work sites, to meet with clients, to pick up supplies, and to negotiate the growth of your business. The deduction for car and truck expenses can be generous, especially under the mileage rate. However, you must keep good, contemporary records that document the trip and the reasoning behind it. Unlike the eras of days past with writing on receipts and calendars, there are now a variety of apps that can ease the burden of tracking mileage, allowing you to record every mile and ensure your deduction is accurate and substantiated.

Tax Tip

To keep your records accurate and complete, update them as you're driving. While you can enter it manually in a paper logbook, we recommend using an online application like those listed above to make it easy and even automatic.

About the Author
Ellie Nava-Jones, EA, MLS

Ellie Nava-Jones is an Enrolled Agent (EA) with BQ Tax & Accounting, a national firm. She received a Master's Degree in English and a second one in Library Science, both from the University at Buffalo, which she put to use in deciphering the Internal Revenue Code. She became an EA to help clients resolve issues with the IRS.

Ellie has been published in several prominent trade journals, academic journals, and books, and has taught for many tax education firms. She enjoys long walks to the fridge and writing terribly dramatic but generic romance novels for fun.

Company: BQ Tax & Accounting, Ltd

Website: www.bqtaxpro.com

Email: ellie@bqtaxpro.com

MISTAKE #9: DEPRECIATION- TOO MUCH OR TOO LITTLE

BY AMBER GRAY-FENNER, EA, USTCP

What is depreciation?

Well, for starters depreciation is the opposite of appreciation. It is the word used to describe the process by which something loses value over time as opposed to gaining value over time. It is also a way of accounting for the wear and tear on an item of property with a useful life of over one year on a business tax return.

The idea that any business expense can be completely "written off" in a given tax year is a common myth and an even more common adjustment when a business return is subject to an IRS exam (audit). The Internal Revenue Code (IRC) and its accompanying regulations spell out in no uncertain terms not only which property can be depreciated, but when property *must* be depreciated. Failing to understand depreciation can be an expensive oversight for small business owners. This chapter provides an overview of the most common depreciation concepts small business owners are likely to encounter.

What Gets Depreciated

Not all business property is able to be depreciated. The first requirement for depreciating property is that the taxpayer generally must own the property. In other words, rented or leased property is not able to be depreciated. Typically, in these cases the rent paid is a business expense.

Of course, this is the IRC so there are exceptions. The most notable exception to the leased property rule is for qualified improvements to certain leased property. For example, certain improvements to a leased warehouse, restaurant, or retail space can be depreciated even though the space itself is not owned by the taxpayer.

To be depreciable the property must be used in the taxpayer's business or income-producing activity (e.g., commercial or residential rental property). In most cases personal use property cannot be depreciated. Certain items often have mixed use for small business owners, the most common being the business owner's car, their home (if they have a home office), and certain items of personal property such as cell phones and computers. Property held exclusively for investment cannot be depreciated.

The property must also have a determinable useful life and be expected to last more than one year. Land, for example, is not depreciable. Even when it is owned by the taxpayer and used in the taxpayer's business, and although it has a useful life of over one year, it cannot be depreciated because it does not wear out, become obsolete, or get used up. Remember, depreciation is a way of accounting for the wear and tear on a piece of property on the tax return. Generally speaking, land is not subject to wear and tear. Neither are "intangibles" such as customer lists, workforce in place, trademarks, patents, and goodwill. Intangibles cannot be depreciated, but they can be amortized as will be discussed later in the chapter.

How Depreciation is Calculated

As mentioned earlier, depreciation is a way of recovering the cost of a piece of property over time (as opposed to all at once) on a business tax return. It is a cost recovery system. The two main types of depreciation small business owners need to understand are straight line (SL) and accelerated.

Real property generally uses straight line depreciation over the life of the property, and a fixed amount is deducted for each year the property is in service.

As the name implies, accelerated depreciation accelerates the cost recovery. It allocates a higher amount of depreciation for the first year and then lower amounts in subsequent years until the asset is fully depreciated. The Modified Accelerated Cost Recovery System (or MACRS) is the depreciation system currently in use for business tax returns.

To fully understand how depreciation is calculated, and therefore its effect on the business tax return, we must understand the following concepts: basis, property type, class life, business use percentage, and date placed in service.

Basis

At its simplest, *basis* is what a taxpayer pays for a piece of depreciable property (cost basis). Basis includes sales taxes as well as shipping and delivery charges. Basis may also include installation and setup charges for the property. Depending on the piece of property, basis may also be adjusted over the course of its useful life.

Adjusted basis includes increases in basis for improvements or additions to the property. For example, a commercial building could have an increase in basis for the costs of bringing electrical or plumbing systems up to code. A work truck could have its basis increased when it is fitted for specific uses such as carrying large windows, having a winch or towing equipment installed, etc. Basis can also be reduced in certain circumstances, one of the most common being when a taxpayer has cancellation of debt income. The taxpayer can sometimes elect to reduce the basis of depreciable assets rather than claiming the cancellation of debt income as taxable.

Adjusted basis is used to determine the gain or loss when a piece of property is traded, sold, or otherwise disposed of. When fully depreciated business assets are sold or traded, the gain on the sale is taxed as ordinary income up to the amount of depreciation taken. Any remaining gain received the more preferential capital gains tax treatment.

For example, a taxpayer purchases a concrete mixer for $5,000. The taxpayer uses the mixer until it is fully depreciated plus a couple of years. The taxpayer then decides to sell the mixer for $500. The taxpayer has $500 of gain taxed as ordinary income. Had the taxpayer sold the fully depreciated mixer for $6,000 the taxpayer would have had $5,000 of ordinary income (the amount of depreciation taken) and $1,000 of capital gain.

Finally, remember that basis for depreciation is sometimes different from the taxpayer's basis in the property and the business' basis in the property for purposes other than depreciation (e.g., distributing it to a partner). It is important to keep track of original cost, basis adjustments, and fair market value at the time property is transferred to accurately determine basis for various cases.

Property Type

In general, depreciable property can be divided into two types: Section 1250 property (real estate) and Section 1245 property (tangible personal property). Remember that "tangible personal property" does not mean personal *use* property but is a type of property other than real estate.

Section 1245 property (tangible personal property)— Section 1245 property is basically anything other than real estate or improvements to real estate. Tangible personal property includes items such as heavy equipment and vehicles, office furniture, computers, appliances, and even livestock and fruit- bearing trees. Typically, the cost basis and class life (discussed in the next section) of these items is relatively easy to determine.

Section 1250 property (real estate)—One of the most common errors for do-it-yourself taxpayers (and sometimes new tax professionals) is not separating land cost from the costs of buildings and other improvements when depreciating real estate. As mentioned above, land is not depreciable property. Nevertheless, the price of the land and the building are often not listed separately when purchasing real property. Cost segregation studies can be done, but often the price of such studies is beyond the reach of small business taxpayers. Sometimes the cost of doing the study is half or more than half of the transaction price. That is simply unworkable. Short of a formal cost segregation study, there is no single right way to isolate improvements from property cost.

One of the most common ways, however, is to look at the property tax assessment or notice of value from the county assessor. Typically, these notices will assign a value to the land and a value to the improvements. Those values can be used to calculate the percentage of value that is land versus the percentage of value that is improvements.

For example, a taxpayer purchases a commercial building and the land on which it sits for $1M. The assessor's notice of value has the assessed value at $500,000 and assigns $375,000 to the building and $125,000 to the land. The building represents 75% of the value, so the calculated basis for depreciation for the building would be $750,000 (75% of the $1M purchase price).

Keep in mind that in many real estate markets the value of the land can far exceed the value of improvements. For example, in

Las Vegas, Nevada, land on "The Strip" is so valuable that buildings are typically destroyed, and a new building constructed rather than trying to conserve a building whose value in relationship to the property is negligible. It works the same for rental real estate in markets such as California. Occasionally owners of rental properties in these areas are expecting a large depreciation deduction for their rental property but once the rental has been divided into land vs building the depreciation deduction is smaller than anticipated.

Certain improvements to land (landscaping, fencing) can be depreciated. Typically, these types of improvements are included in the land basis when originally purchasing a property but are depreciated over their class life (15 years) when placed in service after the property has been purchased. For example, when segregating land from improvements when purchasing a property (and not doing a formal cost segregation study) the value of existing asphalt parking lots, fences, and landscaping would be allocated to the price of the land. If, however, new fencing or new landscaping is installed on a property that is already in use, the improvements can be depreciated over a 15-year class life.

Class Life

To be considered depreciable, an item of property must have a useful life of over one year. For the purposes of depreciation certain types of property are signed into groups and these groups are then assigned a class life. Class life is not the same as useful life. Useful life can vary based on how much or how little a piece of property is used, how hard it is used, or how well it is maintained. Class life is a specified period of time that does not change no matter what state the property itself is in. For example, under MACRS furniture has a seven year class life no matter how long the business owner may use it. Computers and peripherals have a five year class life. The class life for residential real estate is 27.5 years, and for commercial real estate it is 39 years, and their depreciation method is SL.

Date Placed In Service

Finally, when it comes to taxes, timing is everything. Depreciation starts when the asset is placed in service whether it is used or not. If a rental is ready to rent and on the market as a rental on March 1, then that is the date placed in service even if the building is not occupied by a renter until summer. The same thing applies to equipment. If an administrative workstation and computer set up are in place and ready for an employee to use, the depreciation starts when they are ready even if it takes a few months to fill the seat.

In general, it is never a good idea to spend money to save money on taxes. Still, taxpayers often let the tax tail wag the business dog and start "looking for deductions" (e.g., assets to buy) at the end of the year to minimize profits and the associated income taxes. This strategy does not have the desired effect. In most cases (real estate being the notable exception) property placed in service during the year is subject to a half-year convention. The property gets a half year of depreciation if it is placed in service any time during the first half of the year and another half year for the second half of the year (effectively getting a full year's worth of depreciation). Property placed in service any time (beginning or end) of the second half of the year gets 50% of full-year depreciation. But when 40% or more of a taxpayer's depreciable assets placed in service during the year are placed in service during the last three months of the year, it changes the depreciation calculation! Under this particular set of circumstances, a "mid quarter" convention applies to the calculation. Depreciation for property placed in service during the first quarter is calculated as 87.5% of full-year depreciation. Whereas depreciation for property placed in service during the fourth quarter is calculated as 12.5% of full-year depreciation. Depreciation for the second and third quarters are 62.5% and 37.5%, respectively. In other words, trying to back load depreciation by placing assets in service at the end of the year ends up reducing the available depreciation for all assets placed in service during the year and the later the assets are placed in service, the bigger the hit.

Depreciation Alternatives

One of the most common myths of business taxation is the idea that all business expenses are "write offs." The term "write off" is nowhere in the IRC. Rather, the term is short-hand for what may or may not be a deductible business expense—the expectation that (often expensive) assets can be written off in their entirety in a single tax year to minimize taxes. Typically, these items must be depreciated. Of course, as with everything that has to do with taxes and the IRS, exceptions exist. Specifically, there are certain safe harbors and elections that a business owner can make to take a complete write off for an item in a given tax year. Nevertheless, these elections and safe harbors often come with fine print that many people tend to forget about until it's tax time.

Amortization

Amortization is an alternative to depreciation, but it is often not something that can be elected. It is basically a form of SL depreciation where the amortization period is specified by the IRC and or Treasury Regulation. Amortization is most commonly used for "Section 197 intangibles," computer software, and business startup costs.

Section 197 Intangibles

Certain items are neither real property nor tangible personal property but nevertheless are assets owned by the taxpayer, used in the business, with a useful life of over one year. These assets are described by IRC Section 197 (which is where they get their name) and include assets such as customer lists, patents, trademarks, goodwill, value of workforce in place, etc. These assets cannot be depreciated but must be amortized over 15 years (180 months). When purchasing an existing business, taxpayers should take care to segregate the cost of such intangibles from other tangible personal property and real property that is included in the purchase price. And remember, "self-created" intangibles (e.g., copyrighted material, book of business, etc.) are not depreciable, have zero basis and, when sold, will have 100% gain on the sale.

Computer Software—Software (either off the shelf or developed in-house) is another item that is considered "intangible" in regards to depreciation. For software developed in house, the costs could possibly be expensed as R&D expenditures. Alternatively, the costs are amortized over 5 years (60 months) from the date of completion or over 3 years (36 months) from the date the software is placed in service. Commercial off-the-shelf (COTS) software (e.g., accounting, word processing or spreadsheet programs, etc.) is amortized over 3 years (36 months) but is eligible for Section 179 expensing (discussed in greater detail below). Software that is included with the purchase of a computer (installed on the computer when purchased) is included with the computer's depreciable basis and depreciated over the 5-year class life of the machine.

Start-up and Organizing Costs

Often new business owners expect to be able to deduct the expenses related to starting their business. Some even expect to spend money organizing or starting their business in one year in order to incur (and take) a large deductible loss before their business even starts. This strategy is not allowed under the IRC. Typically, start-up and organizing costs are considered capital expenditures and added to the taxpayer's basis in the business.

Taxpayers can, however, elect to deduct up to $5,000 of organizing expenses and/or $5,000 of start-up costs in the year the business begins. The taxpayer can elect to amortize additional expenses in excess of the $5,000 deduction over 15 years (180 months). Organizing expenses include legal fees and accounting, state registration fees, and meeting expenses for board meetings that occur prior to the start of business. Start-up costs include investigating the acquisition of a business, wages paid for staff training, advertising, rent, and payments to vendors prior to opening. Remember, to take the deduction, the business must launch! Exploratory costs for businesses that never open are not deductible. Alternatively, the taxpayer can skip the deduction and elect to amortize all start-up and organizational expenses over 15 years.

Section 179 Election

IRC Section 179 allows a taxpayer to elect to "expense" (take a complete and immediate deduction for) qualifying property.

To qualify the property must be purchased by the taxpayer (it cannot be inherited, gifted, or leased property).

The property must (in general) be tangible personal property (an exception exists for "qualified improvement property").

The property can be new or used and must be used at least 50% in the taxpayer's business.

If business use falls below 50%, a portion of any previously taken depreciation must be recaptured (claimed as ordinary income on the taxpayer's tax return). Common items of property commonly expensed under the rules for Section 179 include cars, trucks, furniture, computers, machinery, etc.

Section 179 expensing is subject to certain limits, the most common being the cost of the items. For 2020, a maximum of $1,040,000 worth of qualifying property could be expensed using Section 179. Further, the maximum deduction cannot exceed the taxpayer's business income. In other words, taxpayers may not use Section 179 expensing to create a loss. The investment income limitation for Section 179 is beyond the scope of this discussion.

Bonus Depreciation

Bonus depreciation is the default tax treatment for all qualifying property. Bonus depreciation of 100% is available for depreciable property placed into service after September 27, 2017, and before January 1, 2023. Bonus depreciation allows the taxpayer to "instantly depreciate" the entire cost of a qualifying asset rather than taking depreciation incrementally over the asset's class life. In terms of income and profit, bonus depreciation has the same tax effects as choosing the Section 179 election. That is, the entire cost of the asset comes off the bottom line in one year.

Unlike Section 179, however, there are no dollar limits on what is eligible for bonus depreciation (except for certain luxury automobiles). Additionally, property purchased from related parties, inherited, or gifted is eligible for bonus depreciation and there is no threshold for business use percentage (and, consequently, no depreciation recapture). Bonus depreciation does, however, instantly and fully depreciate the asset. If the asset is sold, the adjusted basis (due to depreciation) is zero and the gain on the sale will be 100%.

As mentioned, bonus depreciation is the default treatment for qualifying assets. But sometimes a taxpayer may elect out of bonus depreciation. Why? Most often this occurs when an expensive asset is placed into service during an early (or slow) year in the business. The taxpayer may not need the full depreciation deduction in the year the property is placed into service and may want to take advantage of depreciation on the asset in future, more profitable, years.

Safe Harbors and Other Elections

A full discussion of the various safe harbors and elections that exist for certain types of expenditures, and a discussion of the Uniform Capitalization Rules (UNICAP) and the Final Repair Regulations (which spell out what is an expensable repair versus what is an improvement that must be capitalized) is beyond the scope of this chapter. Taxpayers should be aware that the following safe harbors exist for certain types of business expenditures:

- De minimis safe harbor election for acquisitions
- Small taxpayer safe harbor election for improvements

The de minimis safe harbor election allows taxpayers to expense amounts up to $5,000 per invoice or item if the taxpayer has an applicable financial statement (generally one prepared to and attested by a CPA) and up to $2,500 if the taxpayer does not have an applicable financial statement. The election is made for all items of a given class life placed into service in the taxable year. If the election is taken, for example, all 5-year property up to $2,500 per item would be expensed rather than depreciated.

The small taxpayer safe harbor election allows a small taxpayer (defined as $10M or less in gross receipts!) to elect not to apply the UNICAP rules to an eligible building if the total amount paid for repairs, maintenance, improvements, and similar activities does not exceed the lesser of $10,000 or 2% of the unadjusted basis of the building.

. . .

Trade-offs: how to choose the best method

End of (Class) Life Decisions and Depreciation Recapture

When deciding whether and how to depreciate an asset or whether to expense it or use some other alternative method, taxpayers should carefully consider that piece of property's end of life. Depreciation recapture will be a factor if the property is sold or traded in for a new piece of property. It is completely possible to realize a gain on the sale or exchange of used property depending on how long it's been in service and the depreciation already taken. Sometimes, however, no gains are realized. For example, used furniture and office equipment are typically depreciated over five years. These items may be replaced after three years or even after seven to ten years depending on the business owner. If the property is fully depreciated and sold there may be a small gain; however, used furniture and office equipment does not typically hold its value in the same way that other depreciable assets (e.g., heavy equipment or machinery) do. More often, fully depreciated office furniture and computer equipment is simply disposed of. It is either donated or discarded. When this happens, there is nothing to recapture. Business should come, however, be mindful that "discarding" a piece of property by giving it to a shareholder, owner, or partner, could trigger tax consequences for that shareholder, owner, or partner.

If an asset has been expensed using Section 179, instead of being depreciated and the business use percentage falls below 50% the depreciation will have to be recaptured as ordinary income. In other words, if the asset is mixed use (personal and business) the taxpayer should carefully consider the possibility of having to recapture the Section 179 expense. Such scenarios occur frequently with automobiles. Many taxpayers hastily choose the Section 179 election for all or most of their asset purchases without considering the effects of recapture on disposition or a change in business use percentage.

Depending on the asset and its end-of-life factors it may be better, if it qualifies, to choose bonus depreciation over Section 179 expensing.

Section 199A Considerations

Businesses eligible for the Section 199A Qualified Business Income Deduction (QBID) that are also classified as a specified service trade or business (SSTB) may benefit from having assets on their depreciation schedule rather than expensing them. The QBID begins to be phased out for SSTBs that exceed certain income thresholds. The phase outs are extended, however, based on wages paid or the unadjusted basis of assets immediately after acquisition (UBIA). That is, assets on the depreciation schedule may allow for a larger QBID than would otherwise be allowed. Additionally, the UBIA calculation is based on assets placed in service for the preceding 10 years, not on class life. Consequently a 5-year asset that is fully depreciated but still on the depreciation schedule could help a taxpayer who owns an SSTB by increasing their UBIA for purposes of QBID. It sounds like alphabet soup, but it is an important consideration for many small business owners. This is, however, definitely an area where consulting a professional is (strongly) recommended. QBID calculations on SSTBs are not for the faint of heart.

Choosing Not to Decide is Not An Option

A common problem found in do-it-yourself tax returns is failure to depreciate depreciable property. Taxpayers often mistakenly think that by choosing not to depreciate property they can avoid adjustments to basis or depreciation recapture. This is incorrect. Choosing not to depreciate property or simply forgetting to depreciate property is considered an improper accounting method under the IRC if it happens for more than two years. Once an improper accounting method is established it cannot be fixed by simply amending the return to take the omitted depreciation. A request must be made, using Form 3115, to change the improper accounting method to a proper method. The 3115 is a complicated form that requires additional expertise and work from your tax professional, which will cost the business owner more. It's best to choose a correct depreciation method, alternative, or safe harbor the year an item is purchased and placed into service.

While many business owners fear or loathe depreciation, properly used it can be an amazing tax planning tool. Properly timing asset purchases and choosing between depreciation or one of the other alternatives (bonus depreciation, Section 179 expensing, safe harbors, etc.) can help to minimize taxes not simply for one year, but over many years as the business grows and changes. It can help business owners make mindful decisions about whether to discard, sell, or trade their assets. Even the best tax professional in the business does not have a magic wand to make taxes disappear. Proper planning is the next best thing and proper use of depreciation, and its alternatives is one of the most powerful tax planning tools available to the small business taxpayer.

Tax Tip

Depreciation can be a powerful tax planning tool, and if used correctly, can save you money in the first year and for years after the investment.

Keep track of all purchases so depreciation can work in your favor.

About the Author
Amber Gray-Fenner, EA, USTCP

I own Tax Therapy, LLC, in Albuquerque, New Mexico. I am an Enrolled Agent and non-attorney practitioner admitted to the bar of the U.S. Tax Court. I work as a tax general practitioner preparing returns for individuals and (really) small businesses as well as representing individuals before the IRS and the U.S. Tax Court.

My passion is translating "tax speak" into English for taxpayers and tax practitioners and I dispel myths with facts, explaining the 'fine print' behind seemingly simple tax concepts for various global publications. For Forbes.com, I cover individual tax issues and IRS developments with a focus on items of interest to taxpayers and retail tax practitioners. For *ThinkOutsideTheTaxBox.com*, I write about advanced tax planning strategies and pitfalls.

For more about me please visit my website. For more of my writing and insights on current tax policies and events, follow me on Twitter @taxtherapist505.

Company: Tax Therapy, LLC

Website: www.taxtherapy505.com

Twitter: @taxtherapist505

MISTAKE #10: NOT HAVING A USTCP IN TAX COURT

BY LYNN JACOBS, EA, USTCP

Why a Business Might Consider a Tax Court Petition

Generally, the reason to file a petition with the US Tax Court begins with an examination, an employment audit, an income tax audit, or with collection issues pertaining to unpaid taxes.

In examinations, which begin with a letter sent to the taxpayer announcing the audit, the type of return being audited, the year under audit, and the information to be provided to the IRS examiner along with due dates to provide the requested details. During the examination process the IRS examiner reviews the information provided, may request more information, or may close the audit. The closing letter (4549) and included explanations let the taxpayer know whether the examination was closed as a 'no change', or if there is a refund or taxes due.

If the taxpayer (business owner) does not agree with the results they are usually given the opportunity to meet with a group manager, and/or take their case to Appeals. "Appeals is designed to be an independent function within the IRS, completely separate from the compliance functions responsible for collecting and assessing taxes. Appeals provides an information forum for taxpayers who disagree with an IRS determination"[1]. To file for an Appeal the next step is to write down, either in a formal protest or simple statement, the issues with which you disagree and why.

Once the case arrives in Appeals, it will be assigned to an Appeals Officer or Settlement Officer depending on the type of case. The goal is to have the assigned Appeals employee contact the taxpayer by mail or telephone within approximately 30 days of receiving the case; however, it is taking longer these days due to pandemic-related delays and other resource constraints. If an Appeals request has been made and an unreasonable amount of time has passed (more than 120 days), the taxpayer is expected to contact the IRS office to which the appeal request was sent.

In evaluating a case, the Appeals Officer will fully consider the position(s) and argument(s) along with the administrative case file from the IRS compliance person who worked the examination. It is possible to ask to view the non-privileged part of the Compliance file prior to meeting with the office of IRS Appeals. One of the most helpful things one can do is provide all relevant facts, documents and other information supporting the position to the IRS compliance person working the case before it comes to Appeals. If unable to locate an important document that might help explain a certain position, please try to explain the document, why it is not available and what steps were taken to try to obtain copies, etc. In this way, Appeals will have available all the information necessary to fully review the case. Appeals Officers and Settlement Officers try to resolve cases after holding a taxpayer conference or by correspondence. But some complex cases may take more than one conference to resolve.

During the appeal, the Appeals Officer or Settlement Officer will discuss the facts of your case and how the law applies to these facts. Sometimes the facts and tax law are quite apparent. In other cases, the facts may be difficult to tie down, or the law may be open to multiple interpretations. When faced with this type of uncertainty, the Appeals Officer may review court decisions to see how the courts have ruled in similar situations. As mentioned earlier, Appeals may also consider the "hazards of litigation" or the probable outcome if the case were to go to court.

The scope and nature of the Appeals Office review depends on the type of case. But in all cases, the Appeals Officer or Settlement Officer will listen to the taxpayer's concerns and review any comments or information presented before making a final decision. If the case results in a decision felt to be unfavorable, the Appeals Officer will explain the reasons for their decision and any additional options available for resolution. If the taxpayer agrees to settle the case in Appeals, an agreement form will be provided to sign. If the case cannot be settled in Appeals, the taxpayer is entitled to dispute the IRS determination in the Tax Court or another Federal court.

The time it takes for Appeals to work a case depends on several factors, including the type of case, the facts of the case, the complexity of the issues, the availability of legal precedents, other legal theories involved and Appeals' determination of the hazards of litigation. If a petition has been filed with the Tax Court prior to coming to Appeals, that is called a "docketed" case; the time involved will also be affected by dates and timeframes established by the court and beyond Appeals' ability to control. Cases received directly from a compliance function that have not been petitioned to the Tax Court are referred to as "non- docketed" cases. Recently, for non-docketed examination or collection appeals, the entire process, from the time the case is received in Appeals to the time it is resolved or closed in Appeals, takes on average seven or eight months.

In most instances, the taxpayer must have received the so-called '90-day letter' or notice of deficiency (NOD) to file a Tax Court petition. The NOD is called a '90-day letter' as there is a strict 90-day (not 3 months) deadline in which to file a petition with the Tax Court. When the petition is filed the case may be heard as a regular case (may be appealed) or a small case (disputed deficiency under $50,000 but may not be appealed). The petition may be filed by the taxpayer (pro se, i.e., without an attorney), by an attorney admitted to the Tax Court bar or a non- attorney admitted to the Tax Court bar (USTCP).

In the Tax Court Guide for Petitioners, line 5 of the petition asks the taxpayer to tell the Court the reasons for disagreeing with the IRS determination in the case. The errors presumed made by the IRS in the notice of deficiency or notice of determination must be listed clearly and each issue should be listed separately. Briefly state the reasons for disagreeing with the IRS.

For example:

1. I disagree with the IRS's disallowance of the deductions for automobile expenses; the records provided (outside third-party receipts, mileage log) support the deduction.
2. I disagree with the IRS's disallowance of the meals or entertainment expenses; the receipts provided support a deduction.
3. I disagree with the IRS's disallowance of the employee retention credit as all qualifications for that credit have been met.
4. I disagree with the IRS's determination that a levy be imposed on my accounts receivable because: a) such a levy would constitute a financial hardship for my business; and b) because I have proposed an alternative method of paying my federal tax liability.[2]

On line 6 of the petition, you should briefly state the facts to support your position. List each statement of facts in the same order as you listed the issues on line 5. By clearly stating why you believe the IRS is wrong, with supporting facts, you help the Tax Court understand your position.

Lastly, sign your name, preferably in blue ink, on the line for signature of petitioner, along with your position in the business. It is important that each signature be an original signature (and not a copy). Fill in your address and phone number on the lines provided. On the Tax Court website is a page with guidance for petitioners which is very good information for both the taxpayer and their attorney or USTCP.

If one were to review the decisions posted daily on the U.S. Tax Court website the thought often comes to mind – 'what were they thinking? It appears this case has no chance of succeeding and the taxpayer just wants their day in court.' Many taxpayers whose case has no merit (no chance of succeeding) and just want their day in court could be sanctioned by the Judge for filing a frivolous lawsuit. Usually, such a sanction is not imposed the first time a frivolous suit is filed but usually are after the second, third, or fourth such suits are filed. It may take years, though, for that court date to arrive, depending on the circumstances.

Cases filed with Tax Court are given a docket number and tax court date and are again assigned to an Appeals officer. In this writer's experience the tax court date is eight to twelve months after the date the petition was filed.

Many, if not most times, (especially in times Covid-19) the assigned Appeals officer is not in the taxpayer's local area. After a petition is filed with the Tax Court it takes several months before the taxpayer (or attorney) hears from the Appeals officer assigned to the case.

Once the case is assigned to an Appeals officer the taxpayer, or their attorney or USTCP, will be sent a letter with the Appeals officer's contact details, the means by which the conferences will be held (telephone or correspondence via snail mail or fax) and a timeline with deadlines to submit information. In the event no one responds to the Appeals officer's letter, they will call the taxpayer or their attorney or USTCP; this could be months after the initial letter was sent.

In these days of Covid-19 the Appeals officers have an exceptionally large caseload. Mainly this is due to the delays by the IRS in opening their mail and processing the information contained therein. Most IRS employees are in work-from-home status with perhaps weekly office days. The Appeals officer will again ask for your documentation for the issues stated in the petition.

The taxpayer or their attorney or USTCP must be cognizant of specific timelines required to be met. Some due dates begin with the date the petition was filed, and some due dates are worked backwards from the tax court calendar call date.

Those that begin with the date the petition was filed are:

- 60 days after petition – IRS files answer denying the claims (they always deny)
- 45 days after IRS answers – Petitioner replies to IRS answer, or if no reply is required there is an agreement on the issues (joinder of issue)
- 30 days after joinder on issues – formal discovery begins
- Deadlines that are worked backwards from the tax court date are:
- 45 days before calendar call – form discovery ends
- 30 days before calendar call – expert witness reports; motion to continue
- 14 days before calendar call – other pre-trial memos

If both the Appeals officer and the taxpayer come to a meeting of the minds and agree on the issues and their disposition, then the case could be settled before the calendar call or tax court date. If the case is not settled before the calendar call or tax court date then the Court will set a date for a formal trial, usually the week of the calendar call. After the formal trial, post-trial briefs or explanations are filed.

Even after the Chief Judge issues the decision of the court there are further timelines: *90 days after decision issued – the taxpayer could file a motion of appeals to the Circuit Court, unless the case was filed as an 'S' case.*

The decision becomes final when the time period for appeals has closed.

An "S" case is heard under less formal procedures and there is no right of appeal. Cases may not exceed certain monetary thresholds (generally $50,000 per year in issue) to be heard as a small tax case.[3]

No matter what venue an IRS examination takes place, office audit, field audit, correspondence audit, IRS Appeals, Tax Court with assignment to IRS Appeals, the final determination and findings hinge on the quality and veracity of the taxpayer's records. The absolute best defense in any type of examination or proceedings is to have done your 'homework' ahead of time. Make sure that in your everyday business dealings your records are contemporaneously (in the moment) kept. It is so hard to re- create information after the fact.

Seek and heed the advice of your trusted tax professional. While there are many do-it-yourself 'bookkeeping' programs available, business owners should do what they do best – their business. Allow your trusted tax professional the opportunity to do their magic with your business records. Their job is to inform you, the business owner, as to the rules and record keeping requirements. Many tax professionals do bookkeeping and/or accounting for their clients (commonly called write-up work) or have a cadre of qualified colleagues for referral. Allow them to take over the bookkeeping and accounting tasks which would take you away from your business.

Make sure your daily income and expenses are properly noted. There are stricter record keeping requirements for meals and automobile/mileage deductions. Be sure to notate the meal receipts with who, what, where, when, and what was discussed. It is recommended that those receipts that could fade over time be photocopied with the original receipt attached. It is recommended that automobile records include the odometer readings as of the first of the year (1/1/xxxx) and at the end of the year (12/31/xxxx). Be sure to have oil changes and repair work done by an outside third-party to corroborate the mileage details.

Those businesses with employees should be treating employees as such. Discuss with your trusted tax professional the differences between an employee and an independent contractor. These mostly hinge on the issues of control – is the employee or worker told by the employer what to do, how to do it, where to do it, when to do it, and provided the tools to complete the job. If the employer has all (or most) of the control of these issues, then the 'worker' is truly an employee. Make sure all payroll taxes are properly withheld and remitted to the government via EFTPS. File those quarterly reports on time. Timely issue the W2's and W3 to the employees and file them online at Social Security Business Services website.

For those who are truly independent contractors be sure to get the completed W-9 BEFORE paying that person or company. Only by having that completed W-9 in hand will you know whether to issue the tax reporting documents (1099- NEC or 1099-MISC). Track the payment amounts to the independent contractors and issue the 1099-NEC (or 1099- MISC where appropriate) when the amount paid reaches or exceeds the $600 threshold.

As stated earlier, the best defense in any audit, examination, or collection issue is accurate record-keeping as well as prompt payment of all taxes due. Managing these tasks contemporaneously allows one to sleep well at night.

· · ·

History of the U.S. Tax Court

Tax Court was established by congress in the Revenue Act of 1924 as the "US Board of Tax Appeals" and has evolved over the decades to US Tax Court. By an amendment to the IRS Code of 1986, enacted in late 2015, the US Tax Court is deemed to be "not an agency of, and shall be independent of, the executive branch of the Government".[4]

The mission of the United States Tax Court is to provide a national forum for the expeditious resolution of disputes between taxpayers and the Internal Revenue Service; for careful consideration of the merits of each case; and to ensure a uniform interpretation of the Internal Revenue Code. The Court is committed to providing taxpayers, most of whom are self-represented, with a reasonable opportunity to appear before the Court, with as little inconvenience and expense as is practicable. The Court is also committed to providing an accessible judicial forum with simplified procedures for disputes involving $50,000 or less.[5]

Tax Court is a judicial forum that allows for dispute of tax deficiencies (as determined by the Commissioner of the Internal Revenue) without having to pay the disputed amounts before being heard by the court. Jurisdiction includes, but is not limited to, authority to hear:

- Tax disputes on notices of deficiency
- Notices of transferee liability
- Readjustment of partnership items
- Review of failure to abate interest
- Actions for administrative costs
- Worker classification issues
- Review of collection due process cases
- Review awards to whistleblowers

- Enforcement of overpayment decision by the Tax Court if not refunded by the IRS within 120 days after the court decision is final.

In most instances, the taxpayer must have received the so-called '90-day letter' or notice of deficiency (NOD) to file a Tax Court petition. The NOD is called a '90-day letter' as there is a strict 90-day (not 3 months) deadline in which to file a petition with the Tax Court. When the petition is filed the case may be heard as a regular case (may be appealed) or a small case (disputed deficiency under $50,000 but may not be appealed).

Three opinions that can be issued by the Court:

- Bench Opinion – the judge issues an oral opinion during the trial session. Within a few weeks, the taxpayer receives the transcript reflecting the judge's opinion. No precedents are set with a bench opinion.
- Summary Opinion – issued in cases less than $50,000 in dispute; no precedents are set, and this type of decision may not be appealed.
- Tax Court Opinion or Memorandum Opinion – Chief Judge of the Tax Court determines the type of opinion. Memorandum Opinion is issued in a regular case where the law is settled or factually driven. TC Opinion is also issued in a regular case when the Court believes there is a sufficiently important legal issue or principle involved. Both opinions may be cited as legal authority and may be appealed.

Tax Tip

Having an experienced representative is critical when facing Tax Court. And the best defense in any audit, examination, or collection issue is accurate record-keeping as well as prompt payment of all taxes due.

About the Author
Lynn Jacobs, EA, USTCP

 My life as an Enrolled Agent began as a result of my father, David Jacobs, a valuable mentor and a much smarter 'tax man' than I'll ever be! My father passed the EA exam in 1976. I started working for him in 1981 and passed the EA exam in 1989. My father was a member of the inaugural NTPI class, and I am an NTPI Fellow. I passed the rigorous Louisiana civil law notary exam in 2009 and the U S Tax Court exam in 2016. I worked with my father until his death in 1996.

My clientele is diverse and includes a variety of small businesses and self-employed individuals. Our office offers write-up, payroll, sales tax, financials as well as IRS and Tax Court representation, tax return preparation as well as civil law notary services. I have served Louisiana Society of Enrolled Agents as a director, President, Immediate Past President, chaired the website committee and the government relations committee. Service to NAEA include Director, serving on the NTPI Tax Practice subcommittee, the Ethics Committee, Government Relations Committee and Education Committee.

Company: Lynn Jacobs, EA, LLC

Website: www.LynnJacobs-ea.com

Email: lynnjt@bellsouth.net

Phone: 504-469-1025

1. https://www.irs.gov/about-irs/a-closer-look-at-the-irs-independent-office-of-appeals
2. https://www.ustaxcourt.gov/mission.html
3. https://www.ustaxcourt.gov/petitioners_glossary.html#SMALL_TAX_CASE
4. https://en.wikipedia.org/wiki/United_States_Tax_Court
5. https://www.ustaxcourt.gov/petitioners.html

MISTAKE #11: NOT SEEKING TAX PLANNING SERVICES

BY JIM GERNER, EA, CTC

One of your biggest expenses doesn't show up on your profit and loss statement, and that expense is taxes. Indeed, once you make a stable living, taxes will be the largest expense of your lifetime. Since taxes aren't an ordinary expense, it's easy to forget about them when making business decisions.

What might be worse is the anxiety around how the whole process of being taxed takes place. The tax code's vast unknowns can be overwhelming. Taxes are confusing, time-consuming, and can turn into a dark cloud over the head of a small business owner. It's understandable: Your job is to run your business, not to keep up with the ever changing rules and regulations of the IRS.

Don't let that dark cloud sit there because dealing with it seems too daunting. Tackling and understanding taxes is a key factor in running a successful business. In fact, once you are at a certain scale, cutting taxes will be easier than cutting other expenses or adding new revenue, especially with the help of a tax planning professional.

If you have a passive or reactionary relationship with your taxes, now is the time to change that. Leverage the knowledge of a tax professional to actively plan for your taxes and put them to work for you.

The biggest mistake small business owners make is not seeking out tax-related advisory services, whether that's tax planning or coaching. I'm not talking about just finding that extra mileage deduction. That's just doing your tax return. Tax planning is about maximizing what you are doing now to save you in future years.

What Tax Planning is NOT

Tax planning can mean very different things to different accountants, which can cause confusion. Let's clear that confusion by clarifying what we are not talking about first.

We are not talking about just finding more deductions after the fact. Any tax preparer should help you record all your deductions for the prior year. Sure, there are expenses with complex ways to deduct them depending on your business entity. Navigating that maze is part of tax planning, but usually your expenses won't really change.

We are not talking about telling you how much you can put in your IRA. Some tax preparers conflate saving for retirement with tax planning. Certainly, there are advanced retirement vehicles that can be leveraged through tax planning, but in general we are not talking about just saving for retirement in a Traditional IRA.

We are also not talking about simple tax projections. When some accountants offer tax planning services, what they really mean is they offer projection services so you can pay your quarterly or other tax obligations properly. While projecting tax is certainly a necessary first step for tax planning, that is not what we are talking about.

· · ·

So, What is Tax Planning?

It's about decisions. If there's a financial decision to be made, you are doing tax planning, whether you know it or not.

The decision might be, "Should we sell our property?" Or "Should I raise my prices?" For business owners, the stakes are higher because every business decision is a financial decision.

In general, as a Certified Tax Coach (CTC) through the American Institute of Certified Tax Planners (AICTP), a tax planner's goal is to help business owners save real money. Not just defer taxes, project taxes, or find a few extra deductions. This often involves a change in entity type or timing of expenses to create a real dollar savings, either now or in the future. The strategies are varied and nuanced to your situation, and that is why you should hire a professional tax planner to make the best plan for you and your business.

When to Hire a Professional Tax Planner

As a business owner, you should also seek out a tax preparer to help guide you through the tax maze. But sometimes you need to hire someone to do more complex tax planning. Buying, starting, and selling a business are all major financial decisions and all too often the tax professional finds out after they've happened.

Buying or renting out property is another business decision that I often find out about long after the paperwork has been signed. Major purchases are all crossroads that should be navigated with the help of someone who knows how these decisions will impact your taxes.

Outside of these larger business decisions, the question of when you should consider hiring a professional tax planner has an obvious answer: Always!

But what is the best time to engage a professional about tax planning? Not during tax season. It's often too late to capitalize on opportunities as you're looking back at the previous year, and chances are high that your tax preparer is too overwhelmed to do the thorough, thoughtful work required of quality tax planning. Tax season might be the only time you talk to your tax professional, so it can be a good time to start the conversation but know that proper tax planning will happen best at another time.

The end of the year is an appealing time for tax planning because you can see a year's worth of income behind you. This is often another crunch time for the tax professional revving up for a new tax season, and most of the actionable planning won't be able to happen before the end of the year if you start in December. Remember, this is tax planning, not tax rushing at the last minute.

The best tax planning happens in the middle of the year, in June or July, when we have enough revenue for good projections, *and* we have the time to make the necessary changes carefully rather than speed through the process. The follow through should happen in December when we revisit our assumptions with our goals in mind. Finally, your tax savings will be realized during the tax season of the following year and beyond. This sort of planning requires patience and consistent work.

Why You Should Hire a Tax Planner

If you have a small business, you are most likely all too aware of the chiseling effect taxes have on your bottom line. If it's not your biggest expense, it's in the top three. Since you're taxed based on your income, it doesn't show up on income statements. That makes it easy to ignore when you are looking for expenses to cut. Luckily, taxes are one of the key areas where you can cut your costs. Working with a tax professional will ensure you've got a plan to minimize taxes now and into the future.

One would think that here in the age of Google it would be easy to get all of the resources you need to do your tax planning on your own. Nothing could be further from the truth. An internet search in the modern day will lead you down an infinite number of false roads and research mazes. Clients consistently come to me with oddball theories they found by reading and interpreting an article online. It takes a professional to contextualize and analyze tax planning opportunities to decide if they apply to your situation.

As compliance work becomes more and more automated, advisory services are more important than ever. We need tax professionals to get to the heart of the matter.

Who to Hire?

The first step is to find a tax professional you can trust. Ideally, you find a tax professional who knows your industry and who understands where you're coming from as a small business owner. You need someone who won't judge you, and who knows how to see the blind spots and opportunities unique to your industry. Navigating the maze of the tax code with someone who has particular knowledge of your operations, industry and goals makes all the difference.

However, the truth is, many tax professionals are just doing compliance work. They're overwhelmed with tax returns and real planning is never the priority. It's easy to get caught writing a history book rather than choosing your own adventure.

In most states, tax preparers aren't required to be licensed or credentialed in any manner. It may seem ludicrous that in order to cut someone's hair you need multiple years of study, but any person can put up a sign and start a tax business.

However, that's the reality we live in. Since tax preparation and planning is one of the least regulated professions, I'd strongly suggest hiring someone who has credentials.

Keep in mind, while anyone can prepare your taxes, only three types of professionals are authorized to represent you before the IRS:

- A CPA (find one who specializes in taxes)
- An Enrolled Agent, who is a tax specialist
- A tax attorney

So, what should you look for in a tax planner? Most people are surprised to learn that many accountants don't even deal with taxes at all. Even in the world of taxes, no two practices are the same; some tax offices turn out 1040s like a factory, servicing people who are looking to get their refunds quickly, while other CPA firms oversee complex multi-state partnerships. Some tax offices niche down to only help traveling anesthesiologists, for example. You have to be like Goldilocks and put in the time to find the right fit for you.

Find someone who specializes in helping people like you. Tax professionals like to find a niche in a particular industry, so you might be able to find someone who already specializes in preparing taxes in yours. Or maybe you need that personal touch. You might find someone local, so you can meet them in person and establish a relationship. Just make sure they offer advisory services, tax planning, or business strategy. Otherwise, you might have a nice person who can make sure you're compliant, but not someone who can help you realize your goals and see the big picture with a plan for your taxes.

What To Expect When Working with a Professional Tax Planner

As tax planners, it's our job to guide you to the correct route rather than just make sure your governmental requirements are met.

They'll learn your needs.

A plan to save you real dollars, either in the short or long term, depends on your goals.

- Are you looking to retire early and travel the world? Are you building up generational wealth for your family?
- Do you want to sell your business in the next few years? To whom? To a family member? To your employees? To an outside party?
- Do you want or need to save every penny for retirement?

Tax planners worth their salt will learn everything they can about your goals for the future before embarking on your plan.

Without knowing your goals, we can't know the best strategy. Sometimes this will be a clarifying process for you. Maybe you don't know your goals, or at least it isn't what you think about when you're stuck in the day to day of operating your business. Working with a tax planner is a great time to consider the big picture. It's an opportunity to work on your business, not in your business.

What are your personal financial and business goals? Make them big and let us help you take the steps to realize them.

They'll analyze your situation.

A competent tax planner will carefully review and consider your tax documents, needs and goals. We may need more information than is on your tax returns. We take the information you give us and try to find ways to help you. Little things can be important to find that one strategy or loophole that just works for your particular situation.

It pays to be honest with your tax professional. I've had clients who were ashamed of a massive credit card debt, or a gambling habit. Hiding these financial problems is like going to a psychiatrist but withholding the emotions that are troubling you. We are professionals bound by confidentiality (but not attorney client privilege), so put it all out on the table and don't be embarrassed or ashamed. I can almost guarantee your tax professional has seen much, much worse.

They'll find ways to put money in your pocket.

Sometimes there is money just sitting there. There are often credits or opportunities you just haven't taken. The IRS isn't going out of its way to find them for you, and maybe you just need a new set of eyes, or to look in a new direction.

Did you miss any of the pandemic credits? Can you take advantage of changing entity types, accounting periods and methods? Do you have a property that's depreciating over a long period of time that can be accelerated? Can you take advantage of losses from prior years? As a lay person, there is no way to keep track of all of the changing laws, but that's why it's the job of a tax planning professional to analyze all of these opportunities and find the right ones for you.

Every tax plan has hoops to jump through. It's your job to decide whether the costs in terms of time and money are worth the tax savings. It is then also your job to implement the tax plan. The tax planner can only do so much.

When Is It Too Good to Be True?

Sometimes when a tax plan seems too good to be true, it is! If you aren't jumping through hoops and doing a few cartwheels to get your tax savings, there is a good chance it is too good to be true. Check out the IRS Dirty Dozen and of course other sources to see if your tax professional is offering something the IRS has already flagged for fraud. However, many tax strategies are untested in court and there might not be clear guidance. Know your risk tolerance and make sure your tax planner knows your preferences as well. Your tax planner will suggest strategies, but it's always your decision to adopt them.

Sometimes, it seems too good to be true, but it's a legitimate tax savings opportunity (free money!). There are piles of unclaimed stimulus money available to small businesses left-over from the COVID-19 pandemic legislation. Some business owners were shocked to learn they had credits available to cover a large portion of their payroll, well beyond any payroll taxes they paid. These programs seemed "too good to be true" but were legitimate. There are still many governmental programs (not pandemic related) that go unused every day!

When You Need More Than Tax Planning

A tax planner is not the person to consult if you think you might be doing something illegal. I said before that it's always best to be brutally honest about your situation with your tax advisor, but sometimes you just need a lawyer. Tax planners and accountants do not have attorney-client privileges and that protection can only be maintained by a lawyer. While it is against our code of ethics to disclose client information (we wouldn't just report you to the IRS), if compelled by authorities, we cannot offer the same legal protections of a law firm. If you've done something illegal pertaining to taxes (or fear you may have), seek out a lawyer who specializes in taxes.

If you owe the IRS a ton of money and you need to figure out a way to settle the debt, you need another specialist altogether. You need someone who can handle tax resolution with the IRS. This could be a tax planner, but most of the time you will be looking for a CPA, EA or lawyer who specializes in "tax representation" or "tax resolution."

Maybe you are just too small. Most tax planners center their practice around small businesses and people with property holdings. While it's good to have a great advisor, you may not be able to justify the expense of professional tax planning if your net income is under $100K per year. With the S-Corporation not being nearly as beneficial as it once was, you may find some tax professionals who still suggest an S- Corporation at $50K of net income. The truth is the savings may not justify the additional hoops, tax filings and costs associated with an S-Corporation.

You know your industry, and your job. Given the right breaks, your business will be a success. Great! Then Uncle Sam is always there with a hand out for his share. You already endure the day-to-day strains of running your business while juggling a work-life balance. Between Congress changing laws every year, the IRS being almost unreachable for the average person, and the backdrop of unscrupulous tax preparers, it's almost impossible to know how to make a savvy tax plan.

The key is finding a tax professional who is familiar with your industry who you trust and starting that conversation at the right time. If you don't know where to start looking, seek out Certified Tax Coaches (CTC) or Certified Tax Planners (CTP) through the American Institute of Certified Tax Planners (AICTP).

Tax Tip

Not all tax planners have the same experience or credentials so choose wisely. Great tax planners provide you with a comprehensive plan to minimize your tax payments, find unclaimed money, and help you keep more money in your pockets.

About the Author
Jim Gerner, EA, CTC

Jim is an Enrolled Agent and Certified Tax Coach. Jim owns and operates Olympia Tax Service, a full service tax and accounting practice in Olympia, Washington, specializing in tax planning for small businesses, medical professionals, and independent contractors.

Jim Gerner EA, CTC, grew up working in his family's natural foods store in Berkeley, CA. He graduated from reviewing register receipts as a middle schooler to helping run a complex software system during summers home from college. Jim attended Evergreen State College and focused his studies on small business and nonprofit administration. He helped start local nonprofits, most notably a computer recycling and reuse organization that still exists. Jim went to South Puget Sound Community College for classes in accounting and taxes and has been hooked ever since. Professor Gerner now teaches that very same tax class to aspiring accountants and CPA candidates. Jim also develops spreadsheets for other tax professionals to do tax planning. If you're looking for advisory or planning services, please reach out.

Company: Olympia Tax Service

Website: www.olytax.com

Email: jim@olytax.com

Phone: 360-356-7777

MISTAKE #12: NOT PREPARING FOR RETIREMENT

BY PEGGY HASLACH, CFP®, CLU®

"Begin with the end in mind." – **Franklin Covey**

Over the past 10 years, I have met with many entrepreneurs who came to me for small business coaching through my practice and SCORE. When we first sit down to chat, I ask them about their business and their eyes sparkle when they tell me intricate details about their ideas and their plans. Then I ask them to tell me what they want to do with their business when they are done. Do they want to sell it? Do they want to have a family member take over? Do they want to wind down and close the doors? There is always a pause, then various answers that are never as clear or convincing as their opening statements. Then I ask two more questions. How are you going to get from today to that future? And, what are you going to live off of now and in the future? Very few, if any, have the response, "I plan to pay myself first and save for retirement."

Why is that? It is because many business owners are so busy launching their business that they put paying themselves on the back burner. Any money initially earned is put back into the business as they work to scale the business. Then, after a few years when they start seeing a steady stream of revenue, they get that first big tax bill from Uncle Sam. That is when they come back and ask for help.

"My CPA says I need to set up a SEP!"

To this, I reply, "Congratulations! Typically, when someone asks about SEP, or Simplified Employee Pension (SEP), I know their business has reached a point where they could benefit from setting up a SEP... or for that matter a Solo 401(k), SIMPLE IRA, or Keogh plan. Did your CPA mention any of these?"

"Nope, they just said a SEP. And, by the way, what is a Solo 401(k)? Aren't they expensive? I thought only big companies had 401(k) plans."

Before I answer, I ask them "What led your CPA to suggest a SEP?" That's when they tell me that they are paying too much in taxes and are not saving enough for retirement. That is not a bad problem to have and it's likely their CPA thinks their business is generating enough revenue for them to start thinking about ways to save more and reduce their taxes. If that is the case, then a SEP or a solo 401(k) would be beneficial especially if there is only one employee, the practice owner.

The reason that the SEP is always brought up is because they have been around the longest and they are relatively easy to set up. Most financial advisors can set them up in a flash. Solo 401(k)'s or One-Participant 401(k) Plans, as the IRS likes to call them, have a few more rules that prevent financial advisors from suggesting them.

Which is better? It depends.

To establish a retirement plan for yourself or your business, you need to have earned income. One earns income through salaries and wages, commissions, profits from your business and self-employment income. It does not include income from investments or any government program like social security. The amount of earned income you have will also determine how much you can contribute into a retirement plan. For example, if your business generates $2000 in income, the most you can put in any Individual Retirement Arrangement (IRA) is $2000. A CPA is not going to suggest setting up a retirement account until you consistently make and can contribute more than $6000 (or $7000 if you are over 50) to a plan.

I once had a CPA refer a small practice owner to me and when I asked her how much she wanted to contribute to a plan, she said $200 per month. In her case, it made sense to not set up a SEP and she would be better off continuing the contributions to her IRA. On the flip side, another practice owner was told by her husband that she did not make enough money to establish a SEP. With monthly receipts of $12,000 - $20,000, she definitely needed to set up something and at the time, a SEP was the best option. She did and now she is looking to move into a 401(k). There are a few other factors that will determine which is the best starting plan for your business or practice, a SEP or solo 401(k). Let's go through them.

A Simplified Employee Pension plan has many of the same characteristics as a traditional IRA. In fact, it is built on an IRA platform. The funds can be invested in a wide range of assets including stocks, bonds, mutual funds, and exchange traded funds. These accounts can be opened at a bank, brokerage firm, mutual fund company, insurance company or qualified financial institution. The rules for distributions and how the funds are handled in retirement are no different than a traditional IRA. In fact, sometimes the business owner will not have to move the account when they retire or close the business. All they need to do is submit a change request that indicates they will not be contributing so the account's registration should be changed to a traditional IRA.

A SEP is a true profit-sharing arrangement in that the employer contributes the lesser of 25% (or 20% for a sole proprietor or single member LLC) of business revenue or $58000 for 2021 ($61000 in 2022) to themselves and any eligible employee. To be eligible, the employee must be 21, have worked for the employer 3 of the past 5 years and receive at least $650 in paid compensation. If the business has eligible employees, then they must set up and account for each employee and contribute to their accounts every time the owner contributes to their own account. This is usually not an issue, because the accounts are easy to set up and can be established any time before the business files their tax returns (up to and including extensions). Many business owners will work with their CPA and wrap up the entire year's taxes and determine how much the employer should contribute to each account. That flexibility and ease is one of the reasons why practice owners choose to stay with a SEP.

The SEP contribution limits and the fact that the employer must contribute to all eligible employees are the reasons why many business owners move to a Solo 401(k). The Solo 401(k) is for self-employed and owner-only businesses. The business cannot have any full time (1000 hours+) W-2 employees except the owner's spouse if they are working in the business. Because the practice owner wears two hats, employee, and employer, they can make contributions wearing each hat. This allows the owner wearing the employee hat to defer up to 100% of compensation or $19500 in 2021. Then, the owner can put on the employer hat and contribute additional amounts up to $58000 in 2021 ($61000 in 2022). And, if they are over 50 years old, they can tack on an additional $6500 in contributions each year. These contributions can be set up to be pretax, Roth and voluntary after tax.

The SEP on the other hand only allows pre-tax employer contributions. In addition, the Solo 401(k) plans allow participant loans that can have the same terms as regular 401(k) plans. The participants can borrow up to 50% of their balance not to exceed $50K. The term of the loan is 5 years or up to 30 years if the funds were used to purchase a primary residence.

The drawbacks on the 401(k) is that it takes a little more work to get them established and they cost more. Plus, the timeline for setting up the plan is much tighter than a SEP. If an owner wants to make contributions wearing both hats, the plan must be established by December 31, 2021. If that deadline is missed, they will be limited to wearing the employer hat and making a profit-sharing contribution for the year.

To set up a Solo 401(k), the owner will need the help of a Third-Party Administrator (TPA) and a record keeper in addition to a CPA and financial advisor. These roles work together to put together the plan documents and administer the plan. This will cost more than establishing a SEP, but the work is done by the plan professionals and the benefits should outweigh the cost. If they don't, then a SEP would be a better choice. If the owner is on the edge, the determining factor can be their growth potential. If they think they are going to be adding full time employees and may need more tax savings, then a Solo 4010(k) would be a good start.

One of the daunting pieces of a 401(k) is the testing. With a solo 401(k), if there are no employees besides the owner, then testing is not required. The minute employees are hired, then the business must start testing. If these employees meet the plan eligibility requirements, then they must be included in the plan and their elective deferrals (the employee's) contribution will be subject to non-discrimination testing (unless the plan is set up as a safe-harbor plan).

The testing is designed to make sure that employers are not benefitting highly compensated employees more than the rank- and-file employees. To me, that is not a bad thing. The reason is that the business is growing. Moving into a regular 401(k) plan and changing the plan to allow employee contributions, adding a match and other features that would offer the owner additional tax savings. And because all the players are already assembled, it is not that difficult to transition to a regular 401(k).

With a SEP, changing plans requires starting from scratch if the business owner wants to add employee deferrals or the other benefits of a 401(k) or qualified plan.

	SEP	Solo 401(k)
Employer Contributions	YES	YES
Employee Contributions	NO	YES
Who bears investment risk?	Employee	Employee
Maximum ER Contribution	20-25% of revenue	25% of Covered Compensation
Maximum ER Contribution	$58,000	$58,000
Employee Elective Deferrals	$0	$19,500
Catch - up Contribution	$0	$6,500
Roth Contributions	NO	YES
Voluntary Contributions	NO	YES
Loan Provision	NO	YES

The chart above gives some of the key differences between a SEP and a Solo 401(k). There is one final point that should help point you in the direction on which plan is best for your business or practice. A Solo 401(k) plan is generally required to file an annual report on Form 5500-EZ if it has $250,000 or more in assets at the end of the year. A plan with fewer assets and a SEP may be exempt from the annual filing requirement. Nevertheless, with both plans, practice owners should have an annual check-up to make sure their SEP or Solo 401(k) are operating within the rules. This would be a good time to evaluate keeping the plan as it is or moving into a plan that better suits the business.

As I said in the start of the piece, one of the main reasons business and practice owners seek help is because they want to save more and pay less taxes. Adding a retirement plan can help do that and can be a useful tool to grow your business and attract employees. SEPs and Solo 401(k)s are two plans that work well for solopreneurs and one-person practices, but they might not be the right choice for other business entities. Working with a team that can help guide you through all the different types of pension plans, profit sharing plans, deferred compensation plans, and stock plans will allow you to save for the future and avoid taxes in the long run. Isn't that what we all want?

What is the next step?

Many small businesses skip the SEP and Solo 401(k)'s because they start to add employees and want to add a plan where the employees can start saving to their own retirement account. These businesses offer or a SIMPLE IRA (**S**avings **I**ncentive **M**atch **PL**an for **E**mployees) or a basic 401(k) plan. Which plan is chosen depends on who the business owner contacts first for help. Some financial advisors work for big Insurance companies or broker dealers, so set up a SIMPLE IRA using annuities or brokerage accounts. From an advisor's standpoint, SIMPLE IRAs are attractive because they are inexpensive and easy to administer. The employer sets up the plan and has the participating employees work with a financial advisor to set up an IRA account. Then a portion of each paycheck is deposited to the account through payroll deduction. When the payment is processed, the business owner contributes based on the rules of the plan. The contribution the employer makes must be chosen annually and is either:

- 2% nonelective contribution – which means the employer will contribute 2% of the employees' compensation to the SIMPLE account. OR,
- 3% matching contribution-which means matching the employee's contribution dollar-for-dollar up to 3%.

The employer is committed to these plans and may reduce the 3% limit down to 1% if they have some cash flow issues. However, they can only do that 2 out of 5 years.

On the employees' side, the requirements to participate is limited to any employee who received at least $5,000 in compensation from the business during any two preceding calendar years and is expected to receive at least $5,000 in compensation in the current calendar year. The maximum amount an employee may defer is $13500 for 2021 and if they are 50 or over, they can add a $3000 catch up. Like SEP's, SIMPLE plans function like a traditional IRA in terms of the rules for contributions, however, there is one big difference with a SIMPLE, which concerns distributions. If an employee takes a distribution during the first two years of their participation in the plan, they will be subject to a 25% early distribution fee. After two years, the early distribution fee is reduced to the standard 10% if the distribution is taken before they turn 59½.

The SIMPLE also has a unique feature that along with the low contribution levels make it easy for the business to outgrow. Companies that have SIMPLE Plans are not permitted to have any other retirement plan in place. If the owner of a SIMPLE plan wants to maximize deferrals and minimize taxes, they cannot stack or combine it with another plan. Instead, they will have to complete the year and then work with a financial professional to replace the plan with one that is better suited to their needs, like a 401(k) plan.

The 401(k) plan is the most popular type of qualified retirement plan employers offer to their employees. A 402(k) plan is a defined contribution plan where employees contribute a portion of their salaries to a plan where their savings grow tax-deferred. To incentivize employees to save more, employers are given a bigger tax break if they match the employee contributions with a defined amount or couple it with a profit-sharing plan. Because these plans are qualified plan as defined by the Employee Retirement Income Security Act of 1974 (ERISA), they come with a lot of rules and regulations to make sure the plans are compliant, non- discriminatory, and properly funded. The regulations do make the plans more costly to set up and administer, but they also offer both the employer and the employee protections that are beneficial in the long run. They also provide more opportunity to save on taxes.

The key to offering the best plan to your employee and for your business is to pull together a team to help design the plan. This team usually consists of a tax professional (CPA or EA), a third-party administrator (TPA) and recordkeeper, a financial advisor and the business owner, who serves as the fiduciary to the plan. There are some online options that combine the professional roles and provide a DIY option that many are attracted to because it saves them money. These can end up costing the business owner in the long run. Like the SEP and the SIMPLE IRA, these plans are quickly outgrown. Plus, the programs tend to oversimplify the options so that the owner cannot make a mistake when they set up the plan.

What ends up happening is that the employer sets up the plan and inadvertently makes it so that they are contributing only as an employee. They miss that opportunity of donning the employer hat for the increased contributions and tax savings. In addition, when you set up a 401(k) you can add to the plan as your business grows. Online or DIY plans often will not let you add supplemental plans like Cash Balance plans or stock incentive programs.

To illustrate the point let's consider Biz A. They have two owners ages 45 and 50 and five employees. They set up a 401(k) plan with a Safe Harbor Non-Elective Match, which means every employee gets a contribution of 3% of their salary. Looking just at the owners, their contributions are as follows assuming that the owners do the max deferral for 2021 of $19,500 and the 50-year owner can add a $6,500 catch-up contribution.

	Wages	401(k) Deferrals	3% Safe Harbor	Total Contribution
Owner 1 age 45	$50,000	$19,500	$1,500	$21,000
Owner 2 age 50	$150,000	$26,000	$4,500	$30,500
Total		**$45,500**	**$6,000**	**$51,500**

If this employer does not change their plan, their deferrals will be limited by the amounts determined by the IRS and their 3% match will only increase proportionately to their salaries. And since many small business owners try not to give themselves raises, these numbers will stay this way for several years. The good news is that they do get a tax break for contributing a match to each employee, which is helpful if their revenue and, therefore, their taxes are increasing.

Profit-Sharing

The next step would be to add a profit-sharing component. Like the employee match, the profit sharing is distributed to all employees according to a formula, so in our example, we will have each employee getting 5%. The owner's contributions now look like this:

	Owner 1- age 45	Owner 2- age 50	Total
Wages	$50,000	$150,000	
401(k) Deferrals	$19,500	$26,000	**$45,500**
3% Safe Harbor	$1,500	$4,500	**$6,000**
Profit-Sharing (PS) %	5%	5%	
PS Allocation	$2,500	$7,500	**$10,000**
Total Contribution	$23,500	$38,000	**$61,500**

Again, the added contributions to themselves and their employees are not only helpful to increase their contributions, but they also help reduce the taxes for the business as employers are given tax deductions as an incentive for helping their employees save.

This is normally where most companies stop. But if you have a practice where you have highly compensated owners and maybe one or two employees, there is yet another level you can add on to the above plan. That is a Cash Balance Plan.

The example below is an illustration. The actual numbers the owners of a business will have depend upon quite a few variables, like age, number of employees, salary ranges, etc. What is not shown is the cost of administrating plans like this and the actual tax savings. That is why the business owner should enlist the help of retirement plan specialists to work with them to minimize costs (both administration and tax) while maximizing the benefits of having these plans.

	Owner 1- age 45	Owner 2- age 50	Total
Wages	$50,000	$150,000	
401(k) Deferrals	$19,500	$26,000	**$45,500**
3% Safe Harbor	$1,500	$4,500	**$6,000**
Profit-Sharing (PS) %	5%	5%	
PS Allocation	$2,500	$7,500	**$10,000**
Cash Balance % of wages	67%	111%	
Cash Balance Allocation	$33,500	$166,500	**$200,000**
Total Contribution	$54,500	$197,000	**$251,500**

A 401(k) plan, Profit-Sharing, and Cash Balance plan are three examples of plans that can be used as standalone plans or in conjunction with other retirement plans, both qualified (tax advantaged) and non-qualified. A for-profit business might use a 401(k) whereas a tax exempted non-profit might use a 401(b). A company that wants to have employees participate in ownership might adopt a plan that will award employees with stock options or even stock purchase programs. There are quite a few options available as the chart below illustrates:

Qualified Plans		Other Tax Advantaged Plans	Non-Qualified Plans & Deferred Compensation Plans
Pension	Profit Sharing		
Defined Benefit	401(k)	403(b)	ISOs
Cash Balance	Stock Bonus	IRAs	NQSOs
Money Purchase	ESOP	Roth IRAs	ESPPs
Target Benefit	Age- Based PS	SEPS	Rabbi Trust
DB(k)	New Comparability	SIMPLEs	Secular Trust
	Thrift Plans	SARSEPS	Phantom Stock
			Promise to Pay
			Restricted Stock
			457 Plans

What plan is right for your business?

Again, it depends. What is not shown above is the cost of each of these plans. Yes, SEPS and SIMPLES and even employer-sponsored IRAs are a low-cost option for new and startup businesses, but they have limitations. Cash Balance and 401(k) plans might be more expensive to offer, but the tax savings and contributions often outweigh the costs in the long run.

The key is for the business owner to enlist the help of retirement plan specialists, tax professionals, and financial advisors to design plans that work for the business now and will provide the flexibility to grow as these businesses grow. These professionals will know the right plan to help minimize costs (both administration and tax) while maximizing the benefits for the employees and employer. Not only can the owner/employer save for their retirement, but their employees can as well. And the employer can also benefit from the fact that having retirement plans is an employee benefit that will help retain employees and boost morale.

Small business owners put a lot of blood, sweat and tears into building and scaling their businesses. By adding a retirement plan, business owners can benefit both in the beginning phase of their business and after they reach the end.

Tax Tip

Tell your financial advisor how and when you want to exit your business so they can design the best retirement strategies and investment options for you.

About the Author
Peggy Haslach, CFP®, CLU® (she/her)

 Peggy earned her BA in Economics at Stanford and a certificate from San Diego State University in Project Management. She holds her FINRA series 7, Series 66, Insurance producer certifications and Chartered Life Underwriter Designation (CLU®). Peggy also holds her Certified Financial Planner

Designation (CFP®). She is an active member in the Greater Seattle Business Association, GenPride and the National LGBT Chamber of Commerce (NGLCC), where she is certified as an LGBT Business Enterprise. In 2009, Peggy left behind a 23-year career in corporate management to start her own project management consulting business.

In 2013, at age 53, she made a career change when she saw the effect life events had on women's financial security. She realized there were very few female financial advisors who could relate to the different planning needs of women and LGBTQ, providing a more collaborative and educational approach. She is a natural team builder, which stems from being a lifelong athlete in water-polo and swimming. She works collaboratively with her client's other advisors (CPA's, Attorneys, etc.) to create a plan where her clients can make and manage their own money, live the lifestyle they want today and feel confident about their tomorrow.

Company: The Finity Group

Website: www.thefinitygroup.com

Email: peggy.haslach@thefinitygroup.com

Phone: 503-380-0041

CONCLUSION

When your packaging is printed incorrectly, or if your products arrive to your clients late, or if your presentation doesn't land with your audience, you know it and you work really hard to fix those issues fast. Unfortunately, the same is not true for our tax responsibility or our business finances. For many of us, our receipts and records pile up for months or our tax bill sits on our desk unpaid, and only when we are facing fines, penalties, or an IRS audit do we scramble to get on top of the situation.

Our mission in creating this book is to provide you with a valuable resource so you can know your numbers and face any fears around your finances, helping you to take ownership of your success, today and in the future. We don't want to see you stressed, strained, or struggling. We want you to start with the right structures, set up the best systems, and know who to turn to when you want tax strategies to reduce your tax payments and allow you to keep more money in your business and in your bank account.

By covering the top twelve tax mistakes most small businesses make, we are giving you the shortcut to successful tax and regulatory compliance. We covered business entities and structures and business insurance; we introduced you to some of the different professionals who work in the areas of taxes, finances, and the law to help you along the way; we emphasized the power of proper tax planning, as well as examined many of the top traps small business owners fall into when they misclassify employees, over- or under-report expenses or mileage, neglect to build a retirement plan, or don't have proper representation in tax court if it comes to this in your business. If you can avoid these top twelve tax mistakes, your business will no doubt be strong, healthy, and thriving.

We have seen this over and over in every industry: knowing and mastering every part of your business is the most empowering thing you can do to set yourself up for success. And mastery doesn't mean you need to do it on your own; all of the contributing authors work with small business owners just like you to help avoid the most common tax and financial mistakes that cost time, money, and peace of mind. These professionals are here to partner with you and support your business growth.

On the following page, we have listed all of the contributing authors in this book, and their areas of specialty. They know more tax systems, structures, and solutions than you may ever care to know, so invite them to a conversation and see how they can help you and your business.

AUTHOR OVERVIEW

Contributing Author	Area of Specialty
Kevin Barquest	Business Insurance
Jim Gerner EA	Tax Planning Tax Preparation
Amber Gray-Fenner EA, USTCP	Tax Planning Tax Preparation Tax Representation
Shawn Harju	Attorney
Peggy Haslach CFP®, CLU® (she/her)	Financial Advisor
Lynn Jacobs EA, USTCP	Bookkeeping Tax Planning Tax Preparation Tax Representation
Ellie Nava-Jones EA, MLS	Bookkeeping Tax Preparation Tax Representation
Jamie E. O'Kane CPA, CTC	Tax Planning Tax Preparation
Harley Sherman CPA	Bookkeeping Payroll Tax Planning Tax Preparation Tax Representation
Lily Tran EA, CTC, NTPI Fellow	Coaching Bookkeeping Tax Planning Tax Preparation Tax Representation